"THAT THEY MAY HAVE LIFE"
(John 10:10)

35 MEDITATIONS

by

JULIUS D. LELOCZKY, O. CIST.

Foreword by
JOSEPH STRICKLAND
Bishop of the Diocese of Tyler, Texas

Edited by
Jaclyn and Robert Greenfield

En Route Books & Media, LLC
Saint Louis, MO
2021

En Route Books and Media, LLC
5705 Rhodes Avenue
St. Louis, MO 63109

Contact us at **contact@enroutebooksandmedia.com**

Cover Credit: Julius D. Leloczky, O. Cist.

Copyright @ 2023 by Cistercian Abbey, Our Lady of Dallas

ISBN-13: 979-8-88870-067-9
Library of Congress Control Number: 2023943308

All rights reserved. No part of this book may be reproduced, stored in a retrieval system, or transmitted in any form, or by any means, electronic, mechanical, photocopying, or otherwise, without the prior written permission of the author. All biblical quotations are taken from the New American Bible (NAB); the sources of the few exceptions are noted.

Dedicated to my Cistercian Brothers
at the Abbey of Our Lady of Dallas and
at the Cistercian Abbey in Zirc, Hungary

Table of Contents

Foreword by Bishop Joseph Strickland iii

1. A Love Story 1
2. Life 11
3. Ephesians 1:3-10 23
4. Heart of Stone 33
5. Faith 39
6. Advent 47
7. Immaculate Conception 53
8. John the Baptist 59
9. Christmas (1) 65
10. Christmas (2) 71
11. The Holy Family 79
12. The Divine Motherhood of Mary 87
13. Epiphany 95
14. Baptism of Jesus 101
15. Presentation 107
16. Valentine's Day 111
17. Lent 117

18. Prayer 125

19. Do Not Judge 139

20. Holy Thursday 155

21. Suffering 161

22. Easter (1) 169

23. Easter (2) 175

24. Peace 181

25. Black Hole 187

26. Ascension 193

27. Holy Spirit 199

28. Holy Trinity 217

29. Corpus Christi 225

30. Sacred Heart 231

31. Transfiguration 239

32. Assumption 245

33. Christ the King 249

34. Passion 257

35. Death 265

FOREWORD

This timely volume from Fr. Julius D. Leloczky, O. Cist., is a welcome spiritual breath of fresh air. As this text becomes available, we find ourselves in a time in which there is a great need for the spirit of hope and serenity. I'm sure many will find these meditations to be a source of great strength and consolation for these days, for they are a treasury that promises to be timeless. As Father Julius shares his reflections, gleaned as they are from sixty years of priestly ministry, the lasting gift they bring is a deeper connection to Jesus Christ and His Light. Father highlights this through the imagery of the Gospel according to John and the evangelist's use of the terms "life" or "eternal life." At one point he discusses the Incarnation, quoting the German philosopher and theologian Dietrich von Hildebrand: "Everything now bears the mark of the almost inconceivable exaltation of humanity through the Incarnation of God and through the baptism which implants in man a new principle of life, participation in the life of Christ and the Holy Trinity." Just one example of Father Julius' elaboration of this theme which pervades his meditations.

Every age finds itself in need of returning to the roots of Christianity. Father Julius' reflections—inspired by Scripture, some of the great Catholic writings of the late 20th century, and his own experiences—are a true treasure. Optimism is the hallmark of the meditations shared in this book and, after all, that is the attitude that disciples of Jesus Christ must bring to every circumstance.

This volume reminds me of the words of St. Paul in Romans 8, "If God is for us, who can be against us?" This dedicated monk of the Cistercian tradition shares beautiful evidence that rings with the message that truly God is for us. The Lord of life deigns to share his own life with us. I pray that many may have the opportunity to have their journey in Christ nurtured by the reflections of this good disciple.

August 20, 2021, Feast of St. Bernard of Clairvaux

+ Joseph Strickland
Bishop of the Diocese of Tyler, Texas

1

A LOVE STORY

(In place of an Introduction)

My mother was an energetic, vivacious lady. Widowed and retired, she was member of a "seniors" club which she visited almost every afternoon to play cards. On a dark, rainy November afternoon all the seniors at the club looked gloomy, depressed, sad, and lonely. My mother decided that this was not good; in a loud voice she made a suggestion: "Let's sit down in a large circle and, one by one, everybody will tell us the story of his or her first love." All at once, excitement electrified the atmosphere in the room. They arranged the chairs, the ladies put on some makeup, and the gentlemen combed the remainder of their hair. When they sat down, one wonderful story of first love followed the other. That dark, rainy November afternoon became one of the best ever meetings of the club. The story of the first love remains always among the most beautiful memories in every person's life.

The Bible is full of stories of first love. Just take the Old Testament story of Samuel hearing his name called in the middle of the night or the story of the first two apostles of Jesus visiting Him at His lodging. Then later on the brothers Peter and Andrew, James and John experienced an instant love at the invitation of Jesus at the Sea of Galilee. We could list the names of all the great biblical figures. The beginnings of their service of the Lord, for all of them, started with a love story. Take Abraham or Moses, or the prophets Isaiah and Jeremiah. Or Saul-Paul knocked off his horse and hearing Jesus' words, "Saul, Saul, why are you persecuting me?" We can mention also the story of Mary Magdalen, who started out as a prostitute and became the most avid follower of Jesus. And we should not forget the young girl in Nazareth who was greeted by an angel with an *Ave* and who responded with *Let it be*. In all of such stories the first love determined the person's life, and eventually it became a life-long commitment.

Now let me tell you one more such story: the story of my own vocation.

I graduated from high school in June 1950 in communist Hungary, and because of my family's reputation as a reactionary, bourgeois family (my parents owned a French pastry shop, a *patisserie*), I was not admitted to any university. My parents raised me with religion; God was always part of my life. But up to that point, I had been a lukewarm, comfortable Christian. And then, in late August of 1950, something happened. The worst years of communism in Hungary. There was only one political party in the country, the communists, with the occupying Soviet army behind them. There were no private businesses; my family's store was nationalized the year before, forcing my dad and mom to work at menial jobs to put bread on the table. In Budapest a Catholic church was destroyed and on its spot a 40-foot-tall bronze statue of Stalin had been erected as an enormous idol. Cardinal Mindszenty was already in prison, as were thousands of people taken as political prisoners, with hundreds of priests and nuns among them. During the same summer of 1950, all religious orders were suppressed by the

Chapter 1: A Love Story

government, and all priests, nuns, and brothers in a few large monasteries were deported; they suffered in inhumanly crowded conditions. One of the few religious priests who managed to escape the deportation went from town to town and continued to give retreats to young people in secret. He came also to my hometown, Győr, to give a secret retreat. It was to be held at one of the parish rectories. I don't remember how I learned about it, but as soon as I received the news, I knew at the bottom of my heart that I must be there. When it started on a Saturday afternoon, I <u>was</u> there. The participants were about twenty college-age boys and girls. This retreat changed my life.

The true purpose of the retreat was to create in my city a core group of young people who would teach the Catholic faith in secret, "underground," to grade-school children. The organization was built up separately for boys and for girls with two dedicated leaders at the top, a boy and a girl. Pretty soon after the retreat, the groups of children were also formed, and the work of the secret religious instruction started. I was filled with zeal and enthusiasm; the Holy Spirit was evidently working in me. What we did was in outright defiance and resistance to the communist regime. Yet I did not think of and did not mind the evident danger of being arrested and put into prison. I wanted to be an apostle.

During these two years my inner transformation and growth was amazing. I was reading a lot of Catholic literature, and, having acquired a new circle of friends, I had frequent long conversations with them. My mind along with my mental horizon was constantly expanding. My times of prayer were becoming longer and longer and gradually more and more joyful. I was filled with inner joy and peace more intense than anything else I had experienced. Before long, I started to attend Mass also on weekdays. To receive Holy Communion every day became a daily hunger in my soul. I loved to teach religion to my group of children. It was two years later, during the summer of 1952, that the thought first came to my mind that maybe I'd like to do full time what I was doing now part time. It was a vague idea, but gradually a priestly and monastic vocation started to take shape in me. I was glad that this was 100% my idea: no one pushed, coaxed or encouraged me in this direction.

With the arrival of the fall of 1952, a big change happened in my life. My mother was working in a hotel in Győr. There she met one of the cleaning ladies whose son was in a high position in the Ministry of Education in Budapest. By this connection, I was admitted to a two-year college (like a junior college). In early September I moved to Budapest to live with my godparents (a childless elderly couple) and started college life. I enjoyed it in spite of being taught what was mostly nonsensical communist doctrine. But we were also able to read the classics of world literature and that was a great joy.

On the last Sunday of October, the day on which at that time the feast of Christ the King was celebrated, I attended the 11 a.m. High Mass at the University Church. This was the day and this was the Mass during which I received my priestly and monastic vocation. As I was listening to the undulating melody of the Gregorian chant filling the church, all at once the sure awareness descended on me that this is the place where God wants me to be, this is the place where I want to be. A tremendous happiness filled my heart:

Chapter 1: A Love Story

I've found my place in this world; I've found my place in God's Church.

But this was only the beginning. The decision was not so easy to make because I was deeply in love with a pretty brunette girl. The two feelings went side by side in my heart: one time one was stronger, another time the other was. To process and sort out my feelings, to work toward determining what was God's will for me was a long, tough struggle. But by May of 1953, the decision was made: I wanted to be a monk. Not a parish priest, not a missionary, but a monk.

Yes, I wanted to become a monk. But when and where? I had no idea. All religious orders in the country were suppressed. Pannonhalma was the only existing monastery, a Benedictine Abbey, a show-window for visiting Western politicians and journalists to demonstrate the freedom of the Church in Hungary. To enter there was out of question for me: I could not risk increasing my family's bad reputation by entering there openly as a novice. No solution seemed viable.

Then there came the letter from Fr. Detre, a Cistercian priest I knew and was corresponding with. Living in the dispersion, he was working as the organist at a parish. He wrote me that the Hungarian Cistercian Order, although suppressed by the government, continued to exist and even thrive underground. They still were admitting novices in secret. There was no monastery, no uniform, no community; the Abbot, along with dozens of monks, was in prison. The novices lived in the world as students at a university or as civilian workers. They met once a week in secret; nobody was allowed to know about their being Cistercians, not even their own parents. The priest asked me whether or not under these circumstances I wished to join the Cistercian Order. Well, as by then I was a "veteran" of underground church activities, I responded without hesitation, "Yes."

After a month of summer military service, I met Fr. Detre again and just before I went back to Budapest for the second year of college, he gave me this instruction. "Next Sunday evening at 7 p.m., be in the park of Városmajor at the statue of Beethoven. There a middle-aged gentleman dressed in a white suit will be waiting for you. Go up to him and introduce yourself."

The next Sunday was a balmy August evening. The sun was about to set. Indeed, the gentleman in a white suit was there at 7 p.m. at the statue of Beethoven, and we met. He was Father Lóránt 'Sigmond. As I learned later, he was the acting superior of the dispersed Cistercians in Hungary, the vicar of the Abbot when the Abbot had been in prison already for over two years. What followed was a long conversation; it was neither an admission test nor a job interview but rather a friendly exchange, a friendly getting acquainted with each other. It seems Fr. Lóránt liked what I told him because as we parted two or three hours later, he gave me a Budapest address and remarked: "Be at this address next Sunday morning at 9 a.m." This is how my life as an underground Cistercian monk started.

The fall of 1953 was for me a time of great joy and of great sadness at the same time. The great joy was my first contacts with the Cistercian Order as a candidate. And the sadness? One afternoon at the end of September, I received the telegram from my mother: "Your father is dying, come right away." I took the first

Chapter 1: A Love Story

train available and before midnight I was at home in Győr. We had an all-night vigil at the dying bed of my father. He died at about 2 a.m. at the age of 54.

Back in Budapest after the funeral, I spent every Sunday at a family home at Hársmajor street. The generous and brave parents of a Cistercian seminarian gave a room to two Cistercian candidates to live in, and five of us gathered in that little room for an all-day-long study session each Sunday. At noon we prayed the divine office and shared a simple lunch. We studied spirituality, psalms, history of the Order, Rule of St. Benedict, church law, Gregorian chant, and other similar subjects. Various teachers (Cistercian priests) came and went during the day; we remained until evening. Then, late in the evening, we went back to our regular weekday life, jobs or college. The big event, the taking of the Cistercian habit and the official beginning of the novitiate, came in February of 1954. We had a week-long retreat in that small room (during which I skipped my college classes). At its conclusion on a Sunday, in the same little room, we received the white Cistercian habit and celebrated a Mass with Gregorian chant. For about eight hours we were allowed to wear the white Cistercian robes. What a joy! It was on that day during the ceremony that I received also my new secret name, Br. Donatus. We officially became novices of the Cistercian Order. Then, in the evening, we had to take off the white habits, put on the civilian clothes, and go back to our grinding weekday jobs. I remember when I was walking through the snow-covered landscape toward the streetcar stop, I almost burst with joy. I thought, "Now the whole world is white because I became a white-robed novice."

It was hard to keep this joy completely secret; I could not tell anybody the earthshaking event that happened to me. Even my godparents, with whom I was living, knew nothing about my Cistercian connections. I felt I was living a double life, a show-life on the surface, the real one completely hidden in my heart. Only on Sunday in the company of my fellow-novices did I feel that I was in my true habitat, true environment; and, of course, also every morning at the Mass.

Yes, maybe the hardest feature of our hidden Cistercian life was that our <u>real</u> life had to remain a total secret. It was hurting me that I could not tell anything to my mother to whom I was always very close emotionally. She knew only that "something was going on," and this was enough for her. Other young Cistercians were involved in the same organization, just in different small groups, and we did not know anything about each other either. Fr. Lóránt's principle was that the less we knew the better off we were should we be arrested: we could not confess or spill what we did not know.

After another three months of military service, in the fall of 1954 I took my first job as a librarian in the county library at the city of Szombathely. I wanted to find a librarian's job in my hometown Győr to be closer to my recently widowed mother, but I did not get a position there. At a meeting of the communist bosses of the county, the head of the Education Department publicly had stated that this "Leloczky boy" can never work in our county "because he sucked capitalism into himself with his mother's milk."

As the months passed, the time came for my first profession which would end the novitiate and make me officially a professed member of the Cistercian community. This great event took place in September 1955 in Budapest. It was preceded by a weeklong retreat at the very simple summer home of a Cistercian-related family in the hilly Buda side of the city. It was a happy week spent together with Fr. Lóránt and with my novice brothers, a week filled with talks, meditations, divine office, common meals, conversations, and a lot of laughter. The professions were taken by each novice individually. On Friday evening we were sent home, but I was to meet Fr. Lóránt again on Saturday morning in a park at the Buda end of the Margaret Bridge, one of the bridges that connect Buda and Pest over the big Danube River. When we met, Father Lóránt asked me if I had a pen and paper. I didn't, so he sent me to buy some at a stationery store. Then in the park we sat down on a bench, and he solemnly asked me whether I really wanted to be a Cistercian. After my affirmative response he started to dictate in Latin, *"Ego, frater Donatus, promitto tibi."* "I, Brother Donatus, promise you, etc.," the official text of the religious profession and I wrote it down in longhand in ink. At the end I signed the paper as Brother Donatus, my secret Cistercian name. My "civilian" name did not appear anywhere on the sheet, and so, if confiscated by the police, nobody could figure out who wrote it. When we finished, Father Lóránt put away the signed paper and told me, "My son, now you are a Cistercian monk." This was the whole "ceremony" of taking my first vows.

As I look back six decades later, this is the story of the five most important years of my life.

2

LIFE

A little more than twenty centuries ago something unheard of happened. It was actually the greatest event ever since the creation of the cosmos. This event was the Incarnation: when God's Son, the Second Person of the Holy Trinity, took on Himself a human body and soul, and was conceived by and born from the Virgin Mary as the Baby called Jesus in the backward province of the Roman Empire called Israel. When this happened, the Timeless became subject to time, the Unlimited accepted all the limitations of a human person, the Transcendent entered the contingent, and infinite, eternal Love came among us as a newborn Baby. The German philosopher and theologian Dietrich von Hildebrand summarizes this historic event: "Everything now bears the mark of the almost inconceivable exaltation of humanity through the Incarnation of God and through the baptism which implants in man a new principle of life, participation in the life of Christ and the Holy Trinity."

Incarnation is the greatest revolution that has ever taken place on planet Earth. Jesus came not only to heal many sick people and preach about the Kingdom of God: He came to change people's lives in the most fundamental way. He came to share His life with His followers. Upon the creation of the first man and woman, God gave them the ability to receive in themselves something that belongs only to God: His own life. This is the life throbbing at the heart of the Holy Trinity, the infinite life of God that is infinite in every sense of the word, unfathomable, incomprehensible, yes, way beyond the capacities of the human mind, yet given to human beings as a gift, as a grace. The main purpose for which Jesus Christ, the Son of God, God-become-man, came among us was to transmit this divine life to every man and woman of every age in every corner of the planet. We read in the first letter of St. John: "The life was made visible; we have seen it and testify to it and proclaim to you the eternal life" (1 John 1:2); "In this way the love of God was revealed to us: God sent His only Son into the world so that we might have life through Him" (1 John 4:9). Later on, John writes: "God gave us eternal life, and this life is in His Son. Whoever possesses the Son has life; whoever does not possess the Son of God does not have life" (1 John 5:11-12). Nobody can imagine a greater gift than this life. With astonishing boldness, early Christian authors declared that God became man so that man can become God. The "explosion" of the divine life in human nature that revolutionized for ever the existence of human beings on the planet Earth, took place when Jesus, on the third day after His torture and execution, rose from the dead to a glorious new life. As Pope Benedict XVI states in his trilogy entitled *Jesus of Nazareth*, "Jesus's Resurrection was about breaking out into an entirely new form of life, into a life that is no longer subject to the law of dying and becoming, but lies beyond it – a life that opens up a new dimension of human existence" (Part Two, p. 244). The Pope compares this never-heard-of outburst of divine life to an "evolutionary leap." The Pope asks the question: "If there really is a God, is He not able to create a new dimension of human existence, a new

Chapter 2: Life

dimension of reality altogether? Is not creation actually waiting for the last and highest 'evolutionary leap', for the union of the finite with the infinite, for the union of man and God, for the conquest of death?" (p. 247).

In the writings of the Saint John the Evangelist, first of all, but also in the other books of the New Testament Scripture, the words "life" or "eternal life" in most cases refer to this greatest gift of God to humankind. Archbishop Fulton Sheen remarks, "Christianity is not a system of ethics; it is life. It is not a good advice; it is divine adoption." The main purpose of the Incarnation and Resurrection was to bring God's eternal life to earth. Right at the beginning of his gospel, John writes: "What came to be through Him was life, and this life was the light of the human race" (John 1:4). Similarly, the first letter of John begins with these words: "What was from the beginning, [...] the life was made visible; we have seen it and testify to it and proclaim to you the eternal life that was with the Father and was made visible to us" (1 John 1:1.2). Somewhat later, John writes: "God sent His only Son into the world, so that we might have life through Him" (1 John 4:9). The eternal life that has been flowing in infinite abundance from all eternity among the Persons of the Holy Trinity has been brought to earth by the Incarnate Son and is now being lavished on all human beings who open their hearts to it. Jesus declares it openly that His mission on earth has been to pass on the divine life: "I came so that they may have life and have it more abundantly" (John 10:10). This means nothing less than that human beings "may come to share in the divine nature" (2 Peter 1:4). Aware of this mystery, Pope St. Leo the Great shouts out with great joy: "Christian, recognize your dignity and, now that you share in God's own nature, do not return to your former base condition by sinning." Saint Paul teaches the same lesson in different words: "For in Him [Christ] dwells the whole fullness of the deity bodily, and you share in this fullness in Him" (Col 2:9-10). This tremendous gift also gives us the ability to obtain knowledge of God: "Now this is eternal life, that they should know you, the only true God and the One whom you sent, Jesus Christ" (John 17:3). This is what theology calls the mystery of the "indwelling of the divine Persons in us."

To Nicodemus who visited Jesus in secret, during night, Jesus said the well-known words of the verse that, according to Bishop Robert Barron, is the most important verse in the entire Bible and that expresses the truth that gifting the eternal life to the human race has been the main purpose of salvation history: "God so loved the world that He gave His only Son, so that everyone who believes in Him might not perish but might have eternal life" (John 3:16). And the Evangelist John confirms these words, writing: "Whoever believes in the Son, has eternal life" (John 3:36). Faith in Jesus and in the Father is the *sine qua non*, the indispensable condition of receiving eternal life. "Whoever hears my word and believes in the One who sent me has eternal life" (John 5:24; see also 6:47). The other requirement for receiving this life is baptism: "The water I shall give will become in him a spring of water welling up to eternal life" (John 4:14).

When we hear talking about the "eternal life" in St. John's gospel, we may be inclined to think that John means life after death. But no! He is talking about the eternal life brought to earth by

Christ, which every baptized person carries in himself or herself presently here on earth, unless he or she has expelled it by committing a mortal sin. Through the sacraments, first of all through baptism and Holy Eucharist, God's eternal life is streaming in us already now; God's glory is already hidden in us, we carry it in our mortal body, to be revealed fully at the Second Coming of Christ.

But there is much more. Among Jesus' famous "I am" pronouncements, which allude to God's famous name given to Moses, some of the statements identify *life* with Jesus Himself: "I am the bread of life" (John 6:35); "I am the resurrection and the life" (John 11:25); and "I am the way and the truth and the life" (John 14:6); "We are in the One who is true, in His Son Jesus Christ. He is the true God and eternal life" (1 John 5:20). Jesus Himself is the incarnate Life! St. Paul too identifies Christ with life: "When Christ your life appears, then you will appear with him in glory" (1 Cor 3:4). When we receive the divine life at baptism and in the Holy Eucharist, we receive Jesus Christ—and *vice versa*. By receiving baptism and Holy Communion, we are enriched and strengthened with the infinite divine life and are united with Jesus Christ. We are simply inundated by Divinity even as we remain an individual person infinitely loved by God.

By sharing Christ's life, Christians are made brothers and sisters of Jesus, children of our heavenly Father. We are elevated from the status of being God's mere creatures into becoming His beloved adopted children, so much so that we dare to use for God the Father the same name by which Jesus called Him: *Abba*. This means "Father" in Aramaic, in the form by which children call their father: "For you did not receive a spirit of slavery to fall back into fear, but you received a spirit of adoption, through which we cry, *Abba*, Father" (Rom 8:15). Elsewhere, Paul repeats the statement even more clearly: "As proof that you are children, God sent the spirit of His Son into our hearts, crying out, *Abba*, Father! So you are no longer a slave but a child, and if a child then also an heir, through God" (Gal 4:6-7). By pouring into us His own divine life, our adoption as children of God is not a legal fiction but a reality. We are truly and legitimately children of our God the Father!

It's amazing how heredity works in human families, how this mysterious transmission of characteristics from parents to children takes place. Children look like their parents not only in physical appearance but also in their talents and in many other areas. Such a "heredity" should also happen in God's children. We as God's children should put on the features of Christ, who reveals all the perfections of His Father in heaven. In the Sermon on the Mount, Jesus invites His followers to imitate the Father with almost a command: "So be perfect, just as your heavenly Father is perfect" (Matthew 5:48). In Luke's gospel this invitation sounds a little different, emphasizing the Divine Mercy: "Be merciful, just as also your Father is merciful" (Luke 6:36). Echoing Jesus' words, Peter instructs us in his first letter: "Like obedient children, […] as He who called you is holy, be holy yourselves in every aspect of your conduct, for it is written, 'Be holy because I am holy' " (1 Peter 1:14-16). Saint Paul encourages the Ephesian Christians to try resemble to their Creator and Redeemer saying: "So be imitators of God, as beloved children" (Eph 5:1).

Chapter 2: Life

In Greek mythology Prometheus stole fire from Zeus (who hid fire from humans in retribution because of an offense) and brought it back to people on earth. The term *life* in the New Testament can be understood as the divine fire long lost for mankind and given back as a heavenly gift to humanity by Jesus Christ: "I have come to set the earth on fire, and how I wish it were already blazing" (Luke 12:49). The fire that Jesus brought on earth is indeed the eternal divine life, the very life of God, the tremendous, unlimited, unfathomable, timeless loving inner life of God that has been flowing for all eternity among the Persons of the Holy Trinity, in comparison to which our immense universe is only a limited, tiny reality. This life does not belong to human nature: it is a super-natural gift. At the dawn of creation, it was a special grace to the first human beings which, unfortunately, was lost because of their disobedience and their foolish attempt to become their own god. By the Divine Mercy of God, by the Incarnation of the Second Person of the Holy Trinity, the divine life of God entered our created world: Jesus Christ made the greatest gift ever possible available to human beings.

When I am requested to baptize a baby, I am frequently asked why baptism is needed at all for this absolutely innocent little bundle of love. In answer to this question, I explain to parents and godparents and all those present what original sin really is. Original sin is not some kind of a positive thing on the child, like some mud stain on the baby's white robe, that has to be washed off by the sacrament. Original sin is rather something negative, something that is missing in the life of the child: the absence of the eternal life called sanctifying grace, God's own life. The child is in a state of pre-redemption and is in need of the divine life that Christ has brought us by His Incarnation and Pascal Mystery. This is what baptism is: it has the power to bestow us the divine life. This was Jesus' last command to the apostles before His ascension: "Go, therefore, and make disciples of all nations, baptizing them in the name of the Father, and of the Son, and of the Holy Spirit" (Matthew 28:19).

Baptism makes us children of God; by baptism God becomes our *Abba*, our dear Father. Becoming God's adoptive children by baptism, to enter into God's own family, to become members of Christ's Mystical Body the Church is the greatest gift, grace, *charis*, the greatest treasure human beings ever can receive, and the greatest happiness, because we will have this divine life not only during our earthly existence but also in all eternity in heaven. As the priest prays in the Eucharistic Prayer II, "We may merit to be <u>coheirs</u> to eternal life." We inherit eternal life with Christ. This is the wonderful exchange or "commerce" that takes place by the mystery of Incarnation: we human beings grant God our humanity, while God, in return, enriches us with His divinity. We "give" God the ability to suffer and die, and God gives us the potential to live forever as His children. We pray in the Offertory of the Mass for the fulfillment of this mystery: "By the mystery of this water and wine may we come to share in the divinity of Christ who humbled Himself to share in our humanity." The Collect of the Mass on December 17 reiterates the same idea saying: "O God, […] look with favor on our prayers, that your Only-Begotten Son, having taken to Himself our humanity, may be pleased to grant us a share in His divinity."

Chapter 2: Life

"Be holy because I [am] holy" (1 Peter 1:16). We are no longer children of the world as we had been in the past; now we are children of the Father, and so we have to live and act like Him. "It is <u>in Christ</u> that 'the God and Father of our Lord Jesus Christ' chose us 'before the foundation of the world, that we should be holy and without blemish' (Eph 1:4) in His, the Father's, sight" (Bl. Columba Marmion, *Christ, the Life of the Soul*, 3).

Allow me an autobiographic note. Let me describe the moment that Abbot Bl. Columba Marmion and St. Paul's letter to the Ephesians entered my life. I had been a "practicing Catholic" all my life, but right after my high school graduation, in 1950, I was blessed by a second conversion. It started with a retreat, where I became acquainted with some wonderful young people. God used them to grab me and shake me up from the foundation of my existence. By leading me to first-rate Catholic literature, my new friends introduced me to the beauty and wealth of Christian life and teaching. I read voraciously to satisfy my spiritual hunger, but it only increased my appetite. Thus I became acquainted with Abbot Marmion's classic *Christ, the Life of the Soul*, which became one of the greatest reading experiences of my life. The above quote is the opening sentence of the book—which is itself a quote from the letter to the Ephesians. Right at the beginning of his treatise, Marmion introduces the reader to the most fundamental good news of Christianity. He explains that God, in his infinite mercy, not only made the wonderful creature called a human being in His own image and likeness, but He also decided that, above all man's precious faculties, He will give him a share of His unfathomable divine life that cascades eternally among the three Persons of God, the Holy Trinity.

We can find the most dramatic exposition of this mystery, one far beyond the comprehension of any human mind, in Saint Paul's letter to the Ephesians, particularly in its chapter one. What moved me most deeply was right at the beginning of the letter, in verses four and five of chapter one, where Paul writes that God "chose us in Him [Christ] before the foundation of the world, to be holy and without blemish before Him. In love he destined us for adoption to Himself through Jesus Christ" (v. 4). In these two verses Paul tells several earthshaking facts about God. First he says, God "chose us" which means that God knew me personally, a speck of dust in this immense universe. Second, this choosing took place "before the foundation of the world," which means that God knew me even before anything had been created, and thus I was in God's mind from all eternity. He knew me, He planned me billions of years before I ever existed, and He chose me. God chose us, chose me for what? He chose me "to be holy and without blemish before Him [the Father]." God chose me for nothing less but to become holy, to become a saint? This sounds very much like what Jesus said in the Sermon on the Mount: "Be perfect, just as your heavenly Father is perfect" (Matthew 5:48), or like Peter's admonition in his first letter: "As He who called you is holy, be holy yourselves in every aspect of your conduct" (1 Peter 1:15). These words from the New Testament make us recall the famous quote from Léon Bloy, the French Catholic writer of the nineteenth and early twentieth centuries: "There is only one sadness, that of not being saints."

Chapter 2: Life

Calling us to be holy goes together with making us His children and thus giving us the ability to share in the divine holiness. So Paul goes on: "[The Father] destined us for adoption to Himself through Jesus Christ" (Eph 1:5). This adoption, as it was mentioned earlier, is not a legal fiction: God's own life circulates in us as divine blood, which keeps us in constant union with the three Persons of the Holy Trinity. This beatific life is God's greatest possible gift ever given to humankind: "… in accord with the favor of His will," favor meaning the free gift of grace, the sanctifying grace by which we are endlessly connected with our Lord: "In accord with the riches of His grace that He lavished upon us" (Eph 1:7-8).

When I first discovered this most fundamental tenet of the Christian Gospel, I became filled with such strong emotions that I had to leave my home running. At that time I lived in Budapest, the capital city of Hungary. The city is divided into two halves by the Danube River: the western half is called Buda and the eastern half Pest. Buda is hilly, Pest is flat. On the Buda side, right in the middle of the city, on the shore of Danube, there's a rocky mountain called Gellért-hegy. As I was running through the streets, I realized I was actually running up to the top of this mountain, my heart simultaneously filled with a tremendous joy and an immense rage. The joy was caused by learning the first time about my discovery of the mystery that God was pouring His own divine life in me, and the rage was growing in me because of the fact that I had to wait until I was 22 years of age to learn of this mystery for the first time. My mother raised me Catholic, I received a religious education in school for twelve years, I listened to innumerable number of sermons and talks, and yet I never heard about the mystery of God's eternal life overflowing in my soul. On the top of Gellérthegy, looking down over the metropolis below me, I wanted to shout aloud this mystery in everybody's ears: "Brothers, sisters, wake up and realize that you all are God's beloved children, chosen as His own from all eternity!" This was when I became deeply aware, what a tremendous mystery God's grace, God's favor, the sanctifying grace is. Having this sharing of the divine nature (2 Peter 1:4) within us, we can understand that *Parousia* is not some event in the distant future, but that it has already started and we are part of it.

This is the story of how I learned that the term <u>life</u> is one of the most important words in the gospel of St. John and, indeed, in the entire New Testament. This life came from heaven; this divine life revolutionized human existence on earth. Jesus Christ is not only the name of one of the most important persons in history: He has brought God's life on earth, and by this life, He continues to live on the planet Earth in the souls of uncounted millions of people.

3

EPHESIANS 1:3-10

Chapter One of Saint Paul's letter to the Ephesians played not only a vital and enduring role in my spiritual life as such, but also helped me discern my lifelong vocation, God's call for me to become a Cistercian monk. I learned from Ephesians One that God has had a plan, a definite will for my life, and He has had that even before the foundation of the world, and my only chance for a truly happy life is to follow that will. Ephesians One taught me that in a Christian person's life everything is grace, God's unmerited, free favor. This was for me such a cheerful revelation that it gave my whole life a fundamental joy and peace. Let's explore just a few verses of Ephesians One in which St. Paul was teaching about the greatness of a Christian's life and about the *sine qua non,* paramount importance of Jesus Christ in the Christian existence. I limit the analysis only to verses 3 to 10. Let's see some of these blessings.

After a brief opening word of greeting, the letter immediately goes on to the "deep waters" of profound theology of the divine economy of salvation. "Blessed be the God and Father of our Lord Jesus Christ" (v. 3a). The passage starts with a shout of joy, *Blessed be,* similar to Mary's *Magnificat* or Zachariah's *Benedictus*. What is the reason of this great joy? The joy of Virgin Mary or Zachariah was understandable over the great and decisive events of the salvation history; but Paul supposedly wrote his letter locked up in prison cell, looking ahead to a bleak future. These verses are an emotionally overwrought hymn of praise and gratitude of boundless joy; for this reason, we should not expect a precisely ordered description. One thought calls forward the next one, the ideas rush overcrowded on the writer's pen. Why is that great joy?

The address is also solemn and uncommon, "God and Father of our Lord Jesus Christ." Paul calls not on God the Creator of the universe, nor does he mention the traditional Old Testament name of God, "God of Abraham, Isaac, and Jacob." The Old Testament name has a rich and deep meaning because it expresses that the God of the Jews is not the philosophers' abstract, dead concept of God, nor is He similar to the lifeless idols carved of stone or wood of the pagan nations. Rather, He is the living God who called and has taken care of His people for centuries. Paul calls God *Father*, as the Father of "our Lord Jesus Christ." That God is a Father, <u>the</u> Father: this is the great good news of the New Testament. He is Father of Jesus Christ, who is Lord, *Kyrios*, Himself God, through whom God became Father also of the followers, brothers and sisters of Jesus. As Paul writes in the letter to the Galatians, "As proof that you are children, God sent the spirit of His Son into our hearts, crying out, *Abba, Father!*" (Gal 4:6).

Why is Paul blessing God? He blesses God because He "has blessed us in Christ with every spiritual blessing in the heavens" (v. 3b). God be blessed because we have been blessed by Him. The blessing is "spiritual," the working of the Holy Spirit, the presence of the Holy Spirit, so that 1:3 is a Trinitarian formula that expresses the saving act of the Father in the Holy Spirit through Jesus Christ. A little later in 2:6 Paul explains the phrase that this blessing takes place in heaven: "[God] raised us up with Him, and seated us with Him in the heavens in Christ Jesus." The resurrection of Christ means in a spiritual sense also our resurrection, and the glorification of Christ is at the same time also our glorification, as an accomplished fact. Christians are in close connection with heaven, as if already a present reality. The kingdom of heaven is also our kingdom and all its blessings are also ours in Christ, by the love and mercy of God.

"As He [God the Father] chose us in Him [Jesus Christ], before the foundation of the world, to be holy and without blemish before Him [God the Father]" (v. 4). A Christian is a chosen person, chosen even before the beginning of the world. We have been present in God's thoughts even before the creation of the world; He is loving us without any merit on our part, as a good father is loving his child. This choosing happened "in Him," in Jesus Christ, in the only begotten Son of the Father. We are children of God in Jesus Christ; the Father recognizes in us the features of Christ: He knows us only in Him. For what purpose has He chosen us? The purpose was that we would be "holy and without blemish before Him." We read the imperative in the first letter of Peter: "As He who called you is holy, be holy yourselves in every aspect of your conduct, for it is written, 'Be holy because I am holy' " (1 Peter 1:15-16). To be "holy" means to be separated from the profane, sinful world, to be dedicated exclusively to the service of God. We have to be "without blemish" before God, "clean of heart," not by our own merits: this holiness is streaming into us, although our effort is also necessary. This is not an impossible demand since "whoever is in Christ is a new creation" (2 Cor 5:17), united in spirit with Christ, sharing the power of His resurrection.

All this is not some stern military order, not some dry, mindless regulation, but it issues of God's infinite love: "In love, He destined us…" (v. 4-5). Everything that God does or commands happens out of spontaneous love. Love is an eternal, divine quality: "Love never ends" (1 Cor 13:8 RSV); therefore, "…everyone who loves is begotten by God and knows God […] for God is love" (1 John 4:7-8). We are loved by God without limit; we have been continuously in His loving thoughts. He has loving plans for us known by God from all eternity "in accord with the favor of His will."

What is this plan? "He destined us for adoption through Jesus Christ" (v. 5). This is the intention and plan that determines the entire universe, the entire course of world history, everything that is happening to us and around us. Nothing can stand in the way of this plan, except the free will of human beings. Yes, an awesome power, a terrible responsibility, is in our hands: we can frustrate God's plan that was determined by God from all eternity. It depends on our "yes" or "no" response whether God's magnificent plan will be realized in us or not. This is why we have to work on our salvation "with fear and trembling" (Phil 2:12). Yes, indeed: We can thwart God's intention concerning us, although it is an ineffably grandiose plan that we would become God's children through Jesus Christ. Jesus Christ is the Mediator: The plan can be realized only in Him and through Him. He is the only Child of the Father, but the Father wanted this divine sonship extended to every human being. Only Christ is God's consubstantial Son, but God the Father wanted every human being to share in this sonship, every human being to become an adopted child of God. By this adoption, we become God's child not only in name: we share in the divine life, we "come to share in the divine nature" (2 Pet 1:4). In other words, this adoption is much more than the simple outpouring of God's love that every creature enjoys: it is the outpouring of God's own inner Trinitarian life into the human person who wants to receive Him. It is as if adoptive parents could make their adopted child biologically their own offspring. In Christ we become Christ-like indeed, God's beloved child. This assimilation to Christ explains how it is possible that we become "holy and without blemish" (v.4) before God: we put on Christ—"in Him we live and move and have our being" (Act 17:28). This unparalleled and inimitable adoption takes place "in accord with the favor of His will" (v.5). It proceeds from God's eternal loving resolve.

What is the ultimate purpose of this adoption? The ultimate purpose is to do it "for the praise of the glory of His grace that is granted us in the Beloved [Son]" (v. 6). "For the praise": We have been adopted as God's dear children to praise, like Mary in her *Magnificat*, the glory of God and His grace granted to us. As children of God, we are "in Christ." God the Father is loving us as He loves His Beloved Son, with an infinite, limitless love. God intends to confer upon His children a liturgical role that they all join the choirs of angels for a heavenly Divine Office. That we are allowed to praise the glory of God is a free, unmerited gift. In the divine economy everything is grace; we are happy receptacles of God's unfathomable favor. Everything: our election, our invitation for sonship, and our adoption as God's children are sheer gifts, inconceivable divine largesse. Paul mentions this liturgical role of the elect two more times in this chapter. In verse 12, we read, "So that we might exist for the praise of His glory," words that are repeated in verse 14. We find nowhere in the New Testament writings (maybe with the exception of the Book of Revelation) such unequivocal statement that the final and definitive purpose of the entire Salvation History is the eternal praise of the glory of the Triune God by the angels and the elect, His endless liturgical exaltation. "That He granted us in the Beloved [Son]" (v.6.): Christ is again in the center. Christ Himself is the grace personified; "the glory of His grace" is nothing else than Christ's life in us. Christ is the "beloved" Son. "In love" God "destined us for adoption," by which He's loving His "Beloved" Son: In Him God loves the world, in Him did we become the objects of God's infinite love. God is seeing in us the features of His Beloved Son. What a great confidence this awareness can pour into our hearts that God the Father is loving us with the same love by which He loves His Son—that God the Father is loving us because He sees in each of us His only begotten Son!

This infinite love is declared also in the gospel of John in the verse that some authorities consider the most important statement of the entire Bible: "For God so loved the world that He gave His only Son, so that everyone who believes in Him might not perish but might have eternal life" (3:16). Love is not a sweet syrup, but a thing as serious as death. And sin is deadly serious, not just a cosmetic blemish. The Son of God had to shed His blood; He had to die to reconcile us to the Father for our sins. "In Him we have redemption by His blood" (Eph 1:7). Can you fathom what this means, that God Himself had to die so that our sins would be wiped away? That He poured out His blood on the Cross—that His heart pierced by our sins would stop beating!

For the Jews, the idea of redemption had been strictly connected with the memory of their liberation from Egypt. For us Christians, the Jews' liberation from slavery is the paradigm of our liberation from the slavery of sin. This liberation means the "redemption by His blood, the forgiveness of transgressions, in accord with the riches of His grace" (v.7). The weight of sin on one dish of the scale was so heavy that only the total love of the limitless God, the pouring out of His love to the last drop could balance it. This is the overflowing abundance of mercy and grace of which Paul is talking. "Where sin increased, grace overflowed all the more" (Rom 5:20). This redeeming act changed man from God's enemy into God's child. "He lavished on us [the riches of His grace] in all wisdom and insight" (Eph 1:7-8). In a Christian's life everything is grace, which is poured upon us with "all" wisdom and insight, meaning that God's infinite loving wisdom knows no limits. In the eight short verses of our analysis of Chapter One, Saint Paul mentions six times God's immense generosity toward us by terms "blessing," "grace," or "favor." The New Jerusalem Bible interprets Ephesians Chapter One as a set of six great special blessings of God granted to His people.

What is this unbounded, inexhaustible wisdom? "He has made known to us the mystery of His will in accord with His favor…" (v. 9) God "made known to us," He revealed to us "the mystery of His will." The word "mystery" has a long history in the Old Testament, so that in the New Testament literature, and particularly in the letters of Saint Paul, mystery was established already as a technical theological term. It meant God's loving plan of mankind's salvation kept hidden in God's thoughts from the beginning of the world, but now, in this last stage of salvation history, about to be revealed in and by Jesus Christ. This disclosure takes place "in accord with His [Christ's] favor," grace, out of sheer love toward human beings. Just remember Jesus' words: "I have called you friends, because I have told you everything I have heard from my Father" (John 15:15). Out of God's love, we have been made depositaries of His secrets. God included us in the circle of His confidants to whom He wanted to communicate His deepest secrets. This is an added dimension to the mystery of our salvation. Salvation by Christ is not only forgiveness of sins, not even just God sharing with us His divine nature, but it includes knowledge, knowledge of the divine mysteries. These various gifts are intertwined; one is included in the others. Maybe the best example for this is the opening chapter of the gospel of St. Luke in which Zachariah blesses God in his hymn of *Benedictus* for giving "His people knowledge of salvation through the forgiveness of their sins" (Luke 1:77).

What is this ultimate "mystery" of God's will that God has made known to us? "As a plan for the fullness of times to sum up all things in Christ, in heaven and on earth" (v. 10). It has been said that behind the expression of "the fullness of time" the figure of the hourglass emerges by which in Paul's age the time was measured: the "fullness of time" meant when the lower half of the hourglass was full and needed to be turned upside down. In the New Testament scriptures, the "fullness of time" indicated the time

Chapter 3: Ephesians 1:3-10

fixed by God when the prophecies of the Old Testament concerning the Messiah have been fulfilled. In this final time, the time of salvation, according to His plan, God will "sum up all things in Christ, in heaven and on earth" (v. 10). Paul uses here the very complex Greek word *"anakephalaiosastai."* The root of the term is *kephalos,* which means the head, here precisely Christ as head. Thus, the whole enigmatic term communicates that God sums up, recapitulates in Christ as Head of all things in heaven and on earth. This summing up every creature in the world, recapitulation of the entire physical and spiritual universe in Christ, is the ultimate goal of God creating this vast, seemingly endless, yet still limited cosmos, the material world including planet Earth and the human race on it, and the world of all the angelic beings.

4

HEART OF STONE

There's a beautiful German folktale about the heart of stone. Not far from a small town, in the forest, there was a cave and a giant was living in it. This giant had a strange hobby: he was collecting human hearts. Hanging on the walls of his cave, many, many warm human hearts were throbbing. The giant chose as his next victim a young merchant. He arranged an "accidental" encounter with him and promised the merchant great business successes if he visited him in his cave. The merchant was pleased with the offer and followed the giant to the cave. When he entered, he was horrified by the sight of the hanging hearts, but by then it was too late. The giant ripped his heart out of his chest and replaced it with a piece of stone, just as he had done to the rest of his victims.

From this time on, the young man became one of his country's most successful businessmen. Money poured in from every side. But his business transactions gradually became more and more shady. He was cruel, for his heart of stone was unable to feel pity when he saw human needs. But one evening, when he hit his young wife so hard that she fainted, the young merchant came to his senses. Suddenly, he realized that, living as he did, he was destroying his own life and that of his family, and no amount of money could repair it. In the middle of the night, he ran out of the town into the forest and down to the cave of the giant. Once there he tricked the giant into putting back his human heart into his body for just a minute. But when the merchant regained his heart, he slipped out of the giant's hands and escaped from the cave. From that time on his income was smaller, his business did not flourish as splendidly, but he lived happily ever after with his wife.

At the dawn of creation God took a tremendous risk. He created man in His own image and likeness, a being able to think with clarity and make decisions freely. The ultimate purpose for which God created this magnificent creature was that he or she would be able to have a share in the happiness of God's inner, Trinitarian life—the non-stop flow of a tremendous love among the persons of the Holy Trinity. God's original plan, however, was frustrated. The human being misused his free will. He tried to make himself independent of God; he wanted to decide for himself what is good and what is evil. Man made himself his own god. He had sunk into the swamp of his own sins. Toward God he became a rebel, and, as we can see from the story of Cain killing Abel, toward his fellowmen he became cruel, as if he had a heart of stone. Hopelessness became the plight of human race.

The Creator is a stubborn God: He never give up hope. He attempted several times to make covenants with men in order to lure them back to Himself, but their heart of stone drew them back into their sins. Then God decided to perform a radical procedure. He said through His prophet: "And I will give them a new heart, and put a new spirit in them: I will take the stony heart out of their flesh and give them a heart of flesh" (Ez 11:19 RSV). God found a marvelous way to achieve this goal. He sent His only Son among men, and the Son became a man like us, truly one of us. He put the sins of all human beings on the shoulders of His Son, although the Son Himself

Chapter 4: Heart of Stone

was absolutely sinless. All the sins, the whole misery of our heart of stone, became the burden of this one man Jesus, which He carried on His shoulder in the form of a cross. According to St. Paul, "God made the One who knew no sin to be sin, so that through Him we could become God's goodness" (2 Cor 5:21).

Jesus was like an illustration in a medical textbook where in the figure of one human being the artist represents all the possible diseases. Humankind was mortally ill and badly needed surgery in order to replace the heart of stone with a real human heart, so God performed this surgery on His own Son, Jesus. Although the purpose of every surgery is the restoration of the patient's health, not his death, yet, there's no surgery without incision, without blood, without a wound. The surgical intervention for the salvation of mankind took place outside the walls of the Holy City, Jerusalem. Calvary Hill was the operating room, the Cross was the operating table, and the lance of the soldier was the scalpel. Through the passion and death of one man, the heart of stone was removed once and for all from every human being who wishes to live a new, fuller, richer life. On the cross the old, sinful man died, and then this obsolete man was buried. On the third day, in the risen Christ, the whole of humankind rose to new life. The surgery took place on <u>one</u> man, but through it every human being was restored to health who wished to be restored to health. Preface I of the Passion of the Lord expresses this surgery in such words: "For through the saving passion of your Son the whole world has received a heart to confess the infinite power of your majesty." Isaiah writes about this divine surgery: "Yet it was our infirmities that he bore, our sufferings that he endured, while we thought of him as stricken, as one smitten by God and afflicted. But he was pierced for our offenses, crushed for our sins" (Is 53:4-5).

During his life, Jesus called people to himself more than once: "Come to me, all you who labor and are burdened, and I will give you rest. Take my yoke upon you and learn from me, for I am meek and humble of heart, and you will find rest for yourselves. For my yoke is easy, and my burden light" (Mt 11:28-30). But he called in vain, very few came, and those who came just wanted to see His miracles. The true attitude of the people toward Him manifested itself on Good Friday when they shouted with hatred: "Crucify him!"—which meant: This Jesus is disturbing our peace, away with him! Even his closest followers, the apostles, fled. But look, what was the effect of the surgery performed on the Cross! Jesus said: "When I am lifted up from the earth, I will draw all men and women to myself" (John 12:32). He was like a magnet during all His life, but this magnet could not work, because people had hearts of stone, and a magnet does not attract stones. But when He was lifted from the earth up on the operating table of the cross, and the lance of the soldier pierced His heart, then all at once the hearts of all those who were seeking recovery were healed, their hearts of stone were changed into warm, loving, throbbing human hearts, and they allowed themselves to be attracted to Jesus. Just think of the millions of the famous and unknown saints who in the past did allow and today do allow themselves to be attracted to Jesus. Jesus attracted these hearts because they became similar to the Heart of Jesus. This was the divine open heart surgery. This was the way that God achieved our eternal salvation. This is the way that we regained the grace to live as children of God. This is the way that the ultimate friendship between God and we His people has been worked out. Let us look at the cross of Jesus always with the deepest appreciation and limitless gratitude.

Yet we should understand also that the cross of Christ was not only a once and forever remedy for our hearts of stone. As the prophet writes, "More tortuous than all else is the human heart, beyond remedy; who can understand it?" (Jer 17:9). Our hearts remain forever fickle and unsteady: they have the tendency of changing back time and again to be a heart of hard stone. "Oh, that today you would hear His voice: Do not harden your hearts as at Meribah," pleads the Psalmist (Ps 95:7-8). Our volatile hearts need the constant healing presence of the blood-stained cross of Christ glowing gloriously with the splendor of resurrection. In the *Miserere* psalm, the sinner is begging God: "A clean heart create for me, God; renew in me a steadfast spirit" (Ps 51:12). The life of a Christian is a process of repeated conversions, repeated acts of *metanoia,* over and over again. This Greek word *metanoia* means a radical change of heart: the realization that we are walking in the wrong direction, which causes us to stop, turn around, and start walking in the right direction. Of course, we don't do this alone: God's "Divine Mercy" is always with us, and the Good Shepherd does not stop guiding our capricious human hearts.

God never gives up on a soul but He expects that the soul will cooperate with Him. By Jesus Christ, His "self-revelation," He invites us to be His friends, His lover, even His spouse. He's closer to us than we are to ourselves. This level of intimacy is simply unfathomable. This is our vocation; this is our destiny planned by God for all eternity. This is the call for every human being having a "heart of flesh." Is there anything greater, anything higher, anything more appealing a human being could aspire for?

5

FAITH

Helen Keller was born in 1880 in a town called Tuscumbia, Alabama. When she was 19 months old, as a result of an illness, she lost both her vision and her hearing. The blind and deaf little girl had absolutely no contact with the outside world; instead, she was growing up as a little savage in the home of her wealthy parents. She was seven when she received a tutor in the person of Anne Sullivan. Anne figured out an original method to start some kind of communication with Helen. With her index finger she drew the name of everything she showed her on the girl's palm. For a while there was no result. Helen had no idea that words existed, that everything around her had a name. Then one day a miracle happened. Helen herself writes about it in her autobiography: "We walked down the path to the well-house, attracted by the fragrance of the honeysuckle with which it was covered. Someone was drawing water and my teacher placed my hand under the spout. As the cool stream gushed over one hand she spelled into the other the word 'water,' first slowly, then rapidly. I stood still, my whole attention fixed upon the motions of her fingers. Suddenly I felt a misty consciousness as of something forgotten – a thrill of returning thought; and somehow the mystery of language was revealed to me. I knew then that 'w-a-t-e-r' meant the wonderful cool something that was flowing over my hand. That living word awakened my soul, gave it light, hope, joy, set it free!" This was Helen's first escape from total darkness into the light of thoughts. All at once, she had contact with the world. Anne taught her constantly, and Helen, for her part, soaked in the knowledge with her wonderful intelligence. Gradually she became acquainted with Braille, and she also learned to speak. She started to attend school, and eventually she graduated not only from high school but also from university. She became a world famous lecturer, and she dedicated her entire life to the cause of the improvement of the life of blind people. She did all this with Anne's help: Anne Sullivan, the faithful teacher, remained with Helen for the rest of her, Anne's life as Helen's "eyes" and "ears" toward the world.

Antoine de Saint-Exupéry writes in *The Little Prince*: "And now here is my secret, a very simple secret: It is only with the heart that one can see rightly; what is essential is invisible to the eye." The world surrounding us as we perceive it with our senses is indeed, as they say, like an iceberg: what we can see and hear and touch is only a small fraction of all that there is; an infinitely larger part of reality is unapproachable for our senses. This world beyond our perception is the world of God. We all are deaf and blind toward this world, and we would remain deaf and blind always if at one point of our lives a Teacher did not join us so that with His help we would be able to break out of our blind darkness and our deaf silence. This Teacher is Jesus Christ, not a mere human being but the almighty Son of God, second Person of the Holy Trinity through whom God the Father created the universe. Through the help of this Teacher, a new, unknown world opens up for us, a world more real, more durable than the world perceptible by our senses: the world of God's mysteries, the world of God's love, the world of faith. This Teacher, Jesus,

Chapter 5: Faith

who called Himself on one occasion "the light of the world," and at another time "the way, and the truth, and the life," this Teacher gives the same truth and life and light that He Himself is, also to His followers, so that they can say what Helen Keller said: "That living word awakened my soul, gave it light, hope, joy, set it free!"

For a Christian to believe means true light. It means a different kind of certitude that we can obtain by sight or hearing. For a Christian, faith does not mean groping one's way through darkness but rather a new kind of sight in a new kind of light. This new sight is sheer grace, a totally free divine gift which no one can deserve or merit. One who does not receive this gift is unable to believe. Yet even in the one who receives this grace, it does not work automatically. By our own actions, we can strengthen or weaken our faith—for example, by the kind of books we read or by the kind of friends with which we associate. God himself, who gives the grace of faith, frequently tests our faith. There are periods in our lives when it is easy to believe, and there are times when it is difficult. In the difficult times, God allows us to be tempted by doubts, so that our faith, as gold in fire, will be tested and purified. Faith is the gift of Easter: it is the life of the risen Jesus in us. The gift of faith is the first, most fundamental step between God and us, coming even before baptism: for baptism supposes the presence of faith. Let us be grateful for the grace of our faith every minute of our lives.

For Helen Keller, a human being, a <u>person,</u> the person of Anne Sullivan was the one who opened the door for her, Helen, toward objects and persons, toward the understanding of the world, toward the intellectual light. In the same way we are also led by a human being, by a human person, by an all-knowing Teacher, the God-become-man, Jesus Christ, into a new, until-now unknown world. Of course, there is an infinite difference between a human teacher and Jesus Christ as God and Lord. Faith is not an intellectual acceptance of dogmas. Faith first of all and fundamentally is the acceptance of a person, the person of Jesus Christ into my life. First I believe <u>in</u> someone, and only after I have accepted this person into my heart, after I have found him reliable and lovable, will I believe every word of his, everything that he has to say. Faith is an unconditional surrender to another person. True faith is the faith of a high wire acrobat in his companion that he'll catch him in the air, the confidence of an airlines passenger in the pilot that he will take him safely to his destination. True faith is the faith of two friends, of two lovers, of a married couple in each other. Faith is an existential leap, a reaching out toward the other person, and because of this, faith is inseparable from that other existential act that is called love. The two, faith and love, are completely intertwined in the human experience. As love is growing, maturing, changing in me, so is also faith growing, maturing, and changing.

Look at the example of the apostle Thomas. His inner struggle is close to us because it is so typical, so human. It was very human that with his pain over Jesus' death he remained alone. That is why he was not present when the risen Jesus appeared to the apostles for the first time. This was a mistake: He should have remained in the community. In that case he could have seen Jesus sooner. His doubting was also human. He wanted to have certitude: he wanted to be convinced by his own senses that Jesus is alive. And it was human in an exemplary way how, in his shame, he surrendered himself, and how from then on his dedication knew no limits. Thomas was completely disarmed as the risen Jesus turned to him and showed him His wounds. In response, in his profession of faith, he does not say, "You are the Lord, you are God," which would be a simple, intellectual acknowledgement of the divinity of Jesus. Instead, he says: "My Lord, and my God" (John 20:28). He confesses and admits that Jesus became his everything in his life.

Jesus did not limit His teaching to His immediate followers. He was thinking explicitly of the later generations of believers. During the Last Supper He prayed to His Father: "I pray not only for them [the apostles], but also for those who will believe because of their words" (John 17:20). Jesus evidently speaks here about future disciples taught by the apostles. Then, after His resurrection, He said to Thomas: "You believed, Thomas, because you saw me. Happy are those who do not see yet believe" (John 20:29). Here Jesus was talking again about His future followers, the hundreds of generations of Christians – who did not see, yet believed. Ultimately, faith is acceptance of realities not seen.

At one time, Jesus compared the kingdom of God to the dough which a woman mixes with leaven. The leaven penetrates the dough, transforms it, and makes it rise. The dough is the entire Church. Jesus is the leaven. This leaven penetrated first the group of the apostles, then the first generation of Christians, and finally, after the passage of centuries, finally reached us. But even within one person, the work and effort and cooperation with God for an entire lifetime are needed, so that this leaven can work its effect on the whole soul and heart and personality of a human being. The transformation starts with the acceptance of the person of Jesus in faith, and then, through the process of this transformation, every stage, every move, everything depends on faith. Everything depends on the quality and depth of my faith, how much Jesus can suffuse my existence. This means not only my intellect but also my heart, my will, my feelings and emotions, even my body: from this results God's call for sexual purity, whether in married life or in priestly and religious celibacy. What is needed is that we make ourselves available completely to Him, that we place ourselves at His disposal, that we surrender to God our total self, all our talents and abilities, including even the most hidden corners of our personalities. This self-gift to God means as much as if we said to Jesus: "You are the rock foundation of my life, I build my whole life on you; you are my only consolation, the only source of my joy, my closest friend, yes, my spouse." Christian life is nothing else and nothing less than building our whole life on Jesus.

For this reason, the existence of a Christian is always a challenge and a constant scandal for the unbelievers. For them, it is nothing more than the foolishness of the cross, which is scandalous for the Jew and absurdity for the pagan (cf. 1 Cor 1:23). For a person who lived 200 years ago, or even just 50 years ago, to see a person talking in a cell phone would look like a complete nonsense, absurdity. In the same way, for an atheist or an agnostic, the act of prayer is total folly. Yet in reality, with the eyes of faith, this is the only reasonable, logical step that a human being can take, the only road to true happiness. It springs from the discovery of the fact that Jesus is our only resource of strength, the only true goodness worth living for. And this discovery starts at the instant when Jesus, our Teacher, the Rabbi from Galilee, opens for us the world of God that is the world of faith. Everything depends on whether I believe or not. That is why Jesus called happy those who did not see yet believed.

6

ADVENT

The four-week-long season of preparation for Christmas is the season called Advent, the Latin word that means "coming": the coming of the Lord. I remember how, decades ago, as a young seminarian, I was baffled by this period of the year. I was taught that this is a season of waiting for, preparing for, longing after Christ's coming. In the liturgy I heard and prayed the most beautiful expressions of the human soul's calling on the Lord in words and in music, like in the famous "O" antiphons, the seven beautiful prayer-songs which all begin with the letter "O," like the one calling, inviting the Lord: "O come, O come, Emmanuel!"

At the same time, I knew by faith that the Lord is already **here**, for He is with us. He is here among us in the Holy Eucharist and in the other sacraments. He is here in the words of the Bible. He is here in the persons of our neighbors, our confreres, our brothers and sisters. And He is here through the presence of sanctifying grace, God's own life flowing in us, by which indeed "in Him we live and move and have our being," as we read in the Acts of the Apostles (17:28). Jesus Himself declared: "The kingdom of God is [here] among you" (Lk 17:21), and we know that He himself is the kingdom. His last words before His Ascension were: "I am with you always to the end of times" (Mt 28:29). If all these statements are true facts of our faith, why are we still crying to the Lord,

"Come, come?" Is this not a sign of lack of gratitude? God the Father could ask us: "My children, what else do you want? What else could I give you that I have not yet given you? I sent my own Son among you to become one of you, I allowed Him to suffer a terrible death to save you, I raised Him from the dead so that all of you could rise with Him as well, I sent you the Holy Spirit, and you are now the temples of God, the Holy Trinity dwelling within you—what more could you want?"

Only by getting acquainted with the theology of the liturgy did I start to understand that, by celebrating the cycles of liturgical seasons each year, we sacramentally relive again and again all the mysteries of Jesus' life. We begin with the chosen people of the Old Testament waiting for His coming. We continue with His birth in Bethlehem with all its accompanying events until Epiphany, as the great visible manifestation of the invisible God by the mystery of Incarnation, through the Christmas cycle. In a similar way, we re-experience the great happenings of Jesus' suffering, death, resurrection, and glorification through the Easter cycle. As the Church celebrates each episode of Jesus' life, each actually happens again in a mysterious way in us, the members of the Church, Christ's bride and mystical body.

Then I also realized that even in our own lifespan, God is not some static, rigid, and frozen reality within us like a marble statue: He is a living and dynamic God who, although unchanging within Himself, is constantly visiting us with new comings, surprising us by appearing in new forms heretofore unfathomed, in the hour that His older arrivals are fading away in us. It is obvious that my image and experience of God today is different than it was in my

Chapter 6: Advent

childhood, but it is also true that it is different from that of twenty, or ten, or even five years ago. The living God is growing in us, He is always coming closer in a new way, waiting to be admitted more generously into the inner chamber of our hearts. He says to each of us: "Behold, I stand at the door and knock; if anyone hears my voice and opens the door, I will enter his house and dine with him, and he with me" (Rev 3:20). If we try to stick to our old, stiff ideas of God, instead of inviting the living God by calling on Him: "Come!", we may not even realize that we are holding a lifeless idol in our hands, instead of being in the arms of the living God. Just like the waves of the ocean are constantly coming and coming and washing the shore, God wants to visit us constantly with His ever-new arrivals. And all these little visits of God are, ultimately, a part of, foretaste of, and preparation for His future Great Coming at our personal death and at the Second Coming on the Last Day.

Another way to look at the coming of the Lord is to realize that, although God's presence through the sacraments and grace is complete in us, our experience of God's presence can have changes like day gives way to night. God likes to alternate our experience of Him by letting us feel Him at one time present in our soul, at another time absent. A number of years ago the correspondence of Saint Mother Teresa of Calcutta was published in a book, and it was a shock for many readers to learn that this great, saintly lady experienced God's absence in her soul for decades, as if living in constant darkness. This is God's "tough love" way of education: God wants that we love <u>Him</u> and Him alone, not His gifts—like the sweet feeling of His presence. We may experience God's total absence from our lives; this is the experience of the "dark night" of the soul, as St. John of the Cross calls it. The greater the holiness of a person, the darker and longer can be the night in one's heart, as if to make that person feel more like Christ did on the Cross when He cried out: "God, my God, why have you forsaken me!" In the lives of most of us, periods of experiencing at one time the presence of God, and at another time His absence, fluctuate, reminding us always that neither of the two states will last very long, thus we should neither be overjoyed nor sink into despair: that ultimately we should be grateful for both kinds of experiences because in reality God is always close to us and present in our soul.

Of course, God's absence in our life can be caused not only by divine pedagogy but also by our own negligence, by a lukewarm attitude, by living just on the surface of the human experience and being too involved in the affairs of this world. Many people simply ignore God in their lives even if they do not outright call themselves agnostics or atheists. Actually, our post-modern western culture itself can be considered the culture of the absence of God because society has created around us a godless environment. Some time ago, I received an interesting e-mail of a set of pictures of a building. From the outside, the building was a little gothic country church in England. On the inside, the church had been completely remodeled as a comfortable, modern family home. A family bought that unused church and fitted it for themselves as their home. This building could be a perfect image of today's western society.

From the outside, many institutions still resemble a traditional Christian one, but inside nothing remains that would recall their original purpose. The majority of the products of today's entertainment present to us a world and a society entirely void of God. We can see that all around us. With the pretext of not offending people of other faiths, Christian religious faith is in the process of disappearing completely from the life of our society. Christmas itself is becoming more and more a commercial event. We hear non-stop the call: "Shop, shop, shop," while even to mention the birth of Christ is fast becoming a "politically incorrect" attitude. Such a social environment makes Christian living much more difficult than it was decades ago. Of course, people of the "good old times" were not all saints either, and many people sinned, but they knew that they were sinning and eventually they repented. Today people just ask: "Sin? What is it? Does such a thing exist at all?" In older times some people were moral and others were immoral, but today the majority of our society seems to be simply a-moral, with hardly any moral consideration in their minds.

To conclude our reflections, we can say: Yes, it is not only right for us to call God to come to us and among us, but it is a job more important than ever before. Let us call Him and wait for Him longingly to be present in our society, in our families, in our individual souls. For He is the God who will never stop coming to those who call upon Him.

7

IMMACULATE CONCEPTION

Day after day, as we pass through the Christian year, we celebrate the feasts of many saints. How are these saints' feast days chosen? If the day of their death is known, their feast is usually set on the day of their death because it is their birthday in heaven. But in the cases of three select saints, we also celebrate the day on which they were born here on earth. The first one is not difficult to figure out: the birth of Christ the Son of God in Bethlehem, celebrated on December 25th. We also celebrate the conception of Jesus exactly nine months before His birth, on March 25th. We call this day the feast of Annunciation, for it is the day when angel Gabriel announced to Mary that she would be the mother of the Messiah and she conceived Jesus in her womb. The second person whose earthly birthday we celebrate is Mary, and we celebrate it on September 8th. December 8th is nine months before the birthday of Mary, and it is the feast of the Immaculate Conception, when she was conceived by her mother, St. Anne. And the third person is John the Baptist. The gospel of Luke says that Jesus was six months younger than John the Baptist, which means that John's birthday should be celebrated six months before Christmas Day. We celebrate John's birthday on June 24th, also called Midsummer Day.

Why do we celebrate these and only these three earthly birthdays? We do so because only these three persons were born without original sin. Jesus is the all-holy Son of God who came to <u>save</u> us from original sin. As for John the Baptist, we don't celebrate his conception because he was not conceived without original sin: He got rid of original sin (and received sanctifying grace) when Mary, after the Annunciation, visited her relative Elizabeth who was at that time six months pregnant with John. St. Luke writes in his gospel that at the moment when Mary greeted Elizabeth, the baby stirred in Elizabeth's womb. Catholics believe that, while yes, John was conceived with original sin, at the moment of Mary's greeting he was freed from that "stain" and received sanctifying grace

With Mary, the case is different. For all eternity God had planned that at one point of human history a young girl would conceive a baby not by a husband, but directly by the power of the Holy Spirit. This Child would be the Son of God who had lived for all eternity as the second Person of the Holy Trinity and, at one moment of history, by the will of the Father, would come among us as a human being, one like us and one of us. The woman chosen for this unique, all-important, truly earth-shaking task was a young woman in Israel, in the town of Nazareth, in the province called Galilee, and the woman's name was Mary. Because she was chosen to be the new home of the Son of God here on earth, Mary was prepared with the greatest care and in a special way to be a worthy home for Him.

Our first parents, Adam and Eve, by their disobedience lost God's friendship, God's closeness to them, and the special gift of

Chapter 7: Immaculate Conception

divine life: the very life of the almighty triune God called sanctifying grace. They lost it not only for themselves but for all their descendants. Now Mary, the mother of the Son of God, could not be someone who, even for just a moment, was not God's friend or God's beloved child, in other words someone without sanctifying grace. For this reason, God decided to make an exception with Mary, that is, to anticipate the merits of her Son and grant her the grace of Christ's redeeming death and resurrection even before these events had even occurred. Thus He caused her to be conceived by her mother, St. Anne, without the original sin, and it is for this reason we call Mary's conception "immaculate."

Although naming the feast the "Immaculate Conception" is theologically absolutely correct and precise, I feel it is somewhat too negative and too abstract. It tells us what did <u>not</u> happen instead of what <u>did</u> happen at Mary's conception. Remember, in what words the angel Gabriel greeted her: "Hail, full of grace." This greeting tells us positively what actually took place: Mary was completely, totally filled with God's grace from the first moment of her existence so much so that in her soul there was no room for even the tiniest spot of selfishness or sin, no room for the original sin that every other human being inherited from our first ancestors. She was indeed absolutely and completely <u>full</u> of grace.

Thus Mary has been from the first moment of her existence most closely connected and united with God by carrying in her <u>soul</u> God's own life, the sanctifying grace. Similarly, after she conceived Jesus in her womb, she carried in her <u>body</u> the incarnate Son of God. She was the new Temple of God in which the Lord of heaven and earth bodily dwelt. Mary became the obedient New

Eve who, by her total obedience, made up for the disobedience of the first Eve, and gave birth to her Son, the obedient New Adam whose daily bread was to always do His Father's will. This New Adam became the King of God's kingdom who made all men and women who wished to be God's follower the ability to obey Him. Then by faith and by baptism, His followers would receive sanctifying grace and become much more than simple subjects of Christ the King: they become His brothers and sisters and the children of the Father. Now if they are Jesus' brothers and sisters, the mother of Jesus will be also their mother. God gave Mary to us as our immaculately conceived, heavenly mother because He wanted to show that He loves us not only with the love of our Father in heaven but also with the love of a mother. Everything you love in your earthly mother, you will also find in your heavenly mother Mary and more, because she is much more powerful than any mother on earth ever could be. Since she is so close to her Son, her Son cannot refuse anything that His mother asks Him to do, just like He miraculously granted Mary's request at the wedding at Cana. Mary has the greatest, even invincible, power over her Son's heart. Therefore, we can turn to her with all our problems, all our pains, all our needs with confidence and ask her to ask her Son to help us. She will listen to us with a loving mother's heart.

Attributed to the greatest Cistercian saint, St. Bernard of Clairvaux, a beautiful prayer to Mary called the *Memorare* begins with these words: "Remember, O Virgin Mary, that never, never was it known that anyone who fled to your protection or sought your intercession was left without help." Mary is waiting for you, waiting for your prayers, and is ready to help you. You will never get into any difficulty so great that she could not and would not help you: ask her and trust her always.

8

JOHN THE BAPTIST

In the churches of the Greek and Russian Christians, there is a partition, a separating wall right in the middle of the building, separating the sanctuary of the church from the area of the congregation. On this partition there are three doors, and through the wider middle door the faithful can see the altar. The partition itself is beautifully decorated with a number of icons of saints; because of these icons, the partition is called an *iconostasis*. As a rule, on the central spot, right above the middle door, we can see the icon of the Lord Jesus, and to the left and right of Him are the images of Mary, Mother of Jesus, and of John the Baptist. Why does John the Baptist receive such a great honor, greater than for example St. Joseph, the foster father of Jesus, or the chief apostles St. Peter and St. Paul? In so doing, don't our Eastern Orthodox brothers exaggerate somewhat?

Who is this mysterious man standing on the threshold between the Old and New Testaments? We can find in him and in his life several features that make him unique among all the Saints. Let's see seven of them:

1. John is a man filled with joy. Mary, immediately after the Annunciation, traveled in haste to her relative Elizabeth, who was pregnant with John. When Mary greeted Elizabeth, John sensed the presence of the Messiah and stirred for joy in his mother's womb. This joy made him holy and

he became the prophet of joy. God made John a saint even before his birth, set him apart as a special category in the human race, and prepared him to rejoice over the arrival of the Messiah and to proclaim this joy. This joy filled John's heart and soul so much that he did not desire any other joy or consolation in his life. He lived only for this joy: needing nothing else, he resided in the desert.

2. John was the man of the <u>desert</u>. This is what we read in the gospel of Luke: "The child grew and became strong in spirit and he was in the desert" (Lk 1:80). John was most likely raised in the Jewish Essenic monastic community called Qumran, which was in fact located in the desert, close to the Dead Sea. During his earthly life, John was near Jesus only twice: first as an unborn child during the visitation of the Blessed Virgin Mary to Elizabeth, then later in the adulthood when he baptized Jesus. Between these two encounters he spent the long years in the desert where nobody could talk to him except God. He was the saint of the desert because he was the saint of joy. For him the desert was full with flowers, the flowers of spiritual joy. His joy was to listen to the word of God. This is why, through all the Christian centuries, monks have considered John the Baptist as their first and oldest model.

3. John was the <u>witness of light</u>. In the prologue to his gospel, John the Evangelist writes this about John the Baptist: "A man named John was sent from God. He came for testimony, to testify to the light, so that all might believe through him. He was not the light, but came to testify to the light" (John 1:6–8). John the Baptist was the morning

star that can be seen shortly before sunrise. Just like the appearance of the morning star signals the approaching sunrise, John, by his preaching, announced the imminent arrival of the Messiah. His task was to prepare human hearts for the good news of Jesus, and by calling people to do penance he plowed the field of human hearts so that they would be able to receive the seed of the Sower, the words of Jesus. But the only person who can be a witness is one who actually saw the events to which he is testifying. During the years spent in the desert, John received insights into the mysteries of God's plans: this is how he became a witness and why he was sent to tell others what he had seen, how he could recognize Jesus in the crowd and point at him, saying: "Behold, the Lamb of God." But we should not forget that the word "witness" in Greek is "martyr;" John was a witness of the Light not only in his life but also in his death. The violent end of his life (beheading as the price for the dance of a girl) is a prophetic sign, foreshadowing the violent death of the Messiah, the darkest hour of history. John was not only the morning star announcing the nearness of the sunrise; the darkness of his death predicted also the eclipse of the Sun, Jesus Christ.

4. John was the <u>friend of the Bridegroom</u>. Jesus, the One who is to come is not only the Lamb of God who will take away the sins of the world but also the Bridegroom who is coming among us as a human being to betroth to himself the community gathering around Him as His bride: His disciples, His followers, the Church. John the Baptist is the

friend, the best man of this Bridegroom who, according to the customs of biblical times, was supposed to lead the bride to the Bridegroom: "The one who has the bride is the Bridegroom, and the friend of the Bridegroom, who stands and listens to him, rejoices greatly at the Bridegroom's voice. So this joy of mine has been made complete" (John 3:29). John, the man of joy, has found the fullness of his joy upon seeing that the Bridegroom and the bride have met.

5. John was the <u>baptizer</u>. John had a unique task that no human has ever had or will have: He had to baptize with the baptism of penance the One who had no sin. Jesus, who took on Himself all the sins of the whole human race, accepted complete solidarity with sinners when he stepped into the line of people waiting to be baptized by John. This utmost sharing of Jesus in our human plight gave occasion to the descent of the Holy Spirit on Him and the Father's revelation: "This is my beloved Son" (Mt 3:17). John was the instrument of God's hands by which God revealed not only that Jesus is the Son of God, but also that God is a community of three divine Persons: that God is the Holy Trinity.

6. John was a man of <u>obscurity</u>. Immediately after he had finished his mission, John the Baptist disappeared from the scene. The morning star shines in the sky only briefly: in the splendor of the rising sun, it disappears without a trace. This was the manner in which John gave over his place to Jesus. "He must increase, I must decrease." (John 3:30). Once the King has arrived, nobody thinks of the messen-

ger: his role is over. The episode when John sends his disciples to Jesus to find out whether it is really He, truly the promised Messiah who was to come, strikes me as something strange and confusing. Did John in the darkness of the prison lose his clear vision as to who Jesus was? Did he suffer doubts about the true identity of the One whom he called "the Lamb of God?" Imprisoned, at the verge of dying, did God test his faith as well? There is something truly mysterious in the life of John the Baptist. He arrives from the obscurity of the desert, and for a short while he becomes a celebrity, a hero, a prophet—but then he fades again into the obscurity of captivity and violent death. He was the voice crying in the desert. Yes, John was the voice, but (as St. Augustine points out) the Word was Jesus. The voice passes, the Word remains.

7. John was a prophet of Christ's <u>death</u>. John was prophesizing not only by words but also by the ultimate prophetic act, his own death. The Baptist's cruel death by Herod Antipas was a foretelling of Jesus' violent death. John's life indeed ended in a kind of holocaust, a total sacrifice in the service of God. A candle burned down completely and got extinguished. John drank the cup of suffering to the last drop. Remember, he was just 33 years old, six months older than Jesus. He died as the price for the dance of a girl. What a price! By his death, the age of the Old Testament prophets was ended. He lived on the threshold between the two Testaments, and so he was the bridge, the gate between the two. He was the greatest among the Old Testament greats

but the least among the ones in the New (*cf.* Mt 11:11). Even his stature was shortened by decapitation. This was his final confession, his final martyrdom.

*   *   *

After examining the career of John the Baptist we can ask ourselves again: Do the Orthodox Christians really exaggerate by honoring John too much? We have seen that beside Jesus, the Son of God, and Mary the Mother of God, John has indeed a unique role in salvation history. In Jesus' own words, "among those born of women there has been none greater than John the Baptist" (Mt 11:11). With such appraisal from the "highest authority" we can conclude that the honor and veneration given to John the Baptist has never been too much. Only the remark that Jesus added to his praise of John is somewhat disturbing: "Yet, the least in the kingdom of heaven is greater than he" (Mt 11:11). Did Jesus, in saying this, mean us, little, stumbling human beings who dare to call themselves Christians? If there is any greatness in us, <u>that</u> can come only from God. So we can say with St. Paul: "I will gladly boast of my weaknesses, that the power of Christ may rest upon me" (2 Cor 12:9). In that sense we can encourage each other with the encouragement of Saint Leo the Great: "Christian, remember your dignity!" We Christians, even aware of our littleness, we should realize our greatness!

9

CHRISTMAS (1)

A few years ago, during a trip to the Holy Land, a friend of mine purchased a Nativity set. All the figures were there: Jesus, Mary, Joseph, the shepherds with their sheep, the wise men with their camels and gifts. When he arrived at Tel Aviv's Ben Gurion airport for his return trip to America, security was extremely tight. The customs officers checked and X-rayed every item in his luggage, including the Nativity set. They went through each figure, one by one, even the Baby Jesus. "We can't take any chances," one of the officials apologized to my friend. "We have to be sure there is nothing explosive in this set!" Afterward, my friend told me he thought to himself, "If that officer only knew! That one Person in that Nativity set contained the most explosive power in the world!"

The explosive power of the Baby Jesus my friend was talking about is infinitely greater than the combined nuclear power possessed by all the countries of the world. What is this power? It is not the power by which God sent the great flood to punish His disobedient creatures. It is not the power by which He scattered the builders of the Tower of Babel to humiliate a conceited mankind. It is not the power by which He sent earthquake, thunder, lightning and trumpet blast when He descended on Mount Sinai to give His people the Law. The power my friend was talking about is the power Jesus brought with Him into the world on the first Christmas night.

It is a power unlike any other ever known up to that point except the cataclysmic explosion called the Big Bang by which almighty God created the cosmos by simply uttering the words, "Let there be." Only the way the Son of God came into the world He created eclipses the creation of the universe. Jesus came not by a great theophany as described in some of the psalms, nor did He come as a powerful ruler, living in a splendid mansion and served by an army of servants. As others saw it, He came into the world as the son of a poor carpenter, born in a dirty stable, in one of the backward nations on earth subjected to the mighty Roman Emperor. Jesus came into the world just as you and I were born: naked, helpless, fragile, and vulnerable. Like each of us, He had to wait for other human beings to take care of Him; He was completely at the disposal of other people. He grew up and lived as any other poor, simple human being. He knew hunger and He knew thirst. He knew pain. He experienced ridicule. He experienced rejection. He even experienced the worst death anyone could experience—crucifixion.

When the Son of God arrived in the world, he was not greeted by world leaders, by victorious generals or other celebrities, by some important people of the world. Jesus was greeted by smelly shepherds whose earthly status was so low that their testimony was not acceptable in a court of law. When Jesus came into the world, he identified himself with the poor, the suffering, the powerless, the homeless, even the sinful.

The One who was born to a poor couple in a cave used for keeping animals was the Word Himself, who was in the beginning, who was with God and who was God (cf. John 1:1). God Himself visited us as a man; it was the Word who "became flesh and made His dwelling among us" (John 1:14). The great power that Jesus brought into the world is the power that He demonstrated paradoxically in the simple way He lived as a wandering teacher, but He gave a new Law as Moses did centuries before, declaring Himself as "the Lord of the Sabbath" (Mt 12:8), identifying Himself by God's mysterious name given to Moses, "I am" (John 8:58). He was known in Galilee and Judea as the "miracle maker," performing a long set of powerful signs, healings, and other miracles that only God should be able to do. The One, who came to us as a Baby on Christmas night, ended His life on earth also in a paradoxical way, suffering horrendous torture and death by crucifixion. But again, the One, who as the "Suffering Servant" accepted abysmal humiliation at the hands of men whom He had created, as the greatest of His "signs" rose from the dead, experiencing and revealing the highest glorification in history.

Jesus was not a magician or a showman. He did all of this not to elicit people's admiration and praise: The reason why He came among us as a man was not to exhibit His own glory but to make us human beings glorious. He came to take away our ugliness caused by sin and replace it with His own glory. He is the good Samaritan who found us mugged, beaten, and half dead and took care of us, restoring us to health. He is the good father of the prodigal son who with tender love receives His strayed son who has come to his senses and returned home. He came to save us from a sinful state which would have caused us eternal death. The Child of Bethlehem is the Savior of the human race.

God cannot be described in words. He breaks out of the shackles of our human words because words would limit Him. Even the most sublime philosophical definition would be a prison for God. When Moses asked God for His name, God answered, "I am who I am" meaning, "I have no name, I cannot be defined, I cannot be imprisoned in words, my being is unlimited, so do not try to box me up in any name." The Jews, desiring a better name, used God's refusal to give His name as God's name: Yahweh, "I am who I am," or "He who is." The only definition that describes God perfectly was that given by St. John, when he said in his letter, "God is love." Love is an accurate description of God because love by its very nature is universal, unlimited, all-inclusive. St. Bernard, the great Cistercian saint, says that "the measure of love is that it has no measure." Love is so much God's quality that He can be identified with love. Every true love comes from God. And Christmas is the night when Love was born on our Earth. Christmas is the night of the explosion of Love.

If you admit Christmas into your heart, you admit Love into your heart. Yes, the Law was given already before Christmas: "Love the Lord your God with all your heart, with all your soul, and with all your strength," and "Love your neighbor as yourself." These words are from the Old Testament. The Law was there but people were not able to keep it. Of course, God-sent leaders like Abraham, our father in faith, had a glimpse of what true love really is. However, Abraham, along with Moses, the great liberator of his people; Samuel, the last of the Judges; the long-suffering Job, Elijah, Elisha and the other great prophets; and then, at the threshold of the New Testament, John the Baptist merely foreshadowed the new age brought into being on Christmas. Most people Jesus

Chapter 9: Christmas (1)

found around Himself in the Holy Land were either sinners, like the tax collectors and prostitutes, or self-righteous Pharisees and self-seeking Sadducees who, as Jesus saw it, were farther away from God than the sinners. Men and women were longing after true love and companionship but they could not find it. Without Christ there was no real closeness, no real love. People lived in isolation because they had not met Christ and were unable to love with the love of Christ.

Even today, many people live in such isolation. Is there any way to get out of this icy, dark loneliness? Yes, there is, but only through Christmas, only through Christ, only if we allow Christ to enter our lives. Since Christ's time there have been many millions of famous and unknown saints who testified to Christ's love, loved God totally, and loved their neighbor selflessly. All this love comes from the manger of Bethlehem. Christmas has brought into our world the explosion of love. Now, through Christ, there can be communication between God and man. Christ is our "Jacob's ladder" to make this communication possible. And there can be communication between people. Christ is our cell phone that connects people and creates between them a communion in love. This being-together with God and with our friends, following Christmas, is a permanent, habitual reality. We are with God not only when we actually pray: we _live_ in His presence wherever we are and in whatever we do, except when we sin. Our friends, both those deceased and those who are alive, are present to us not only when we are physically close to them. Love keeps us close to each other. We live in their presence always when love fills our hearts. Only hatred, criticism, and uncharitable thoughts cut us off from them.

"God is love," and true love keeps us permanently in the company of God and of all those whom we love. "No one has ever seen God, but if we love one another, God lives in union with us, and his love is made perfect in us" (1 John 4:12). There is no loneliness for us Christians. When a Christian is by himself, he lives in a solitude that still includes a lasting communion with God and with all those he loves.

Thus we have the tools, we have the opportunity, and we have the gift of communication: now it is our job to continue Christmas, carry the spark in our hearts, and make the miracle of Christmas present wherever we are.

10

CHRISTMAS (2)

It is an interesting, uplifting truth that Christmas can change the human heart. We see it time and again that the birth of a Child some 2000 years ago in a faraway country unexplainably transforms people and makes them gentle and considerate toward each other. How does this miracle happen?

Our story tonight takes us back to the Battle of the Bulge of WWII during the winter of 1944–45. In December, in the forests of the Ardennes plateau heavy fighting was raging between Nazi Germany and the Allies. Between the two fronts, in the middle of the thick, snowed-in woods, there was a little house in which a German woman lived with her young son. She had heard no news concerning her husband who had been drafted long ago and was fighting in the war. The wintery forest provided some semblance of protection and plenty of firewood, but the roar of the approaching fighting became louder and louder. Then late one evening the front door opened and there appeared on the threshold three American soldiers. All three suffered from frostbite, and one of them was badly wounded and bleeding. For a moment the woman was scared, but then she signaled them to come in and sit down. With the fine sense of a housewife, she knew what she had to do.

She collected ingredients for a meal from her modest supplies and began to cook dinner for her unexpected guests.

She knew that the Nazis would give her the death penalty for what she was doing. While she was working, she heard knocking again at the front door. Now four German soldiers stood at the open door. Everyone froze. What would happen next? The woman jumped between the two groups of soldiers. "There will be no shooting here," she shouted in a firm voice. The newcomers quietly came in, leaned their weapons against the wall, and sat down.

The warmth of the stove and the aroma of the meal being prepared slowly melted the tense atmosphere. The men, supposedly enemies, began to speak with each other in a mix of English and German. It turned out that two of the four German soldiers were only 16 years old. Their sergeant, with his 23 years of age, was the oldest among them. In civilian life, he had been a medical student. While dinner was being prepared, he bandaged the wounded American and tended to the others' frostbite. Then the woman put the food on the table, stood with folded hands, and said grace before the meal. The battle-hardened soldiers bowed their heads to hide their tears. They all thought of their families far away. Outside of the house, the noise of the war continued to rumble, but these men in this little house in the middle of the forest made their separate peace treaty.

Without knowing it, they had followed the Star. It was Christmas night, 1944. The Child, the Prince of Peace, was born. In the morning, the soldiers said good-bye to each other with a handshake. The German sergeant, who knew the territory, lifted his

Chapter 10: Christmas (2)

arm and pointed in a direction. The Americans understood. They saluted and started walking toward their unit.

Once again, the question: What does it mean that at Christmas people become nicer, that at the time of the birth of the Child of Bethlehem the ice thaws on human hearts, and they become able to give presents, to be kind and generous—that, in spirit, they even become little children again? The birth of Jesus creates this revolution of hearts. But we can ask: why do we limit this revolution of hearts only to Christmas? Jesus does not leave us after Christmas night: He remains with us throughout the entire year! Why cannot we remain kind and selfless and considerate to each other every day of the year, not only at Christmas? People around us are starving for a tender, friendly word: why do we deprive them of it? It would take so little an effort to say a good word: why don't we give it?

Christmas is not just one day in the endless series of days that zoom by us: It is much more than that. The event of the Incarnation was the greatest, most shocking happening in the history of the world, an unheard-of event that makes Christmas the axle around which all the other days of the year rotate. At Christmas, with the birth of the Child of Bethlehem, eternity entered time, eternal life broke into the small, fragile human life and changed the meaning of all times, gave a new meaning to each of our days. We should celebrate Christmas throughout the year, leaving behind the externals, stressing the essentials. Each of us should bring to victory in our environment the revolution of hearts that the birth of Jesus has brought on earth.

What is the true gift of Christmas? I'd answer this question in three short sentences:

1. Christmas makes us into children of God;
2. Christmas makes us brothers and sisters to each other; and
3. Christmas changes the entire material world into a divine reality.

Let us look at these gifts one by one:

1. We are children of God already by the simple fact that He created us. But God also gave us a much more wonderful way to become His children. When the Son of God became a human being, He made every man and woman on earth His brother and His sister if they are baptized and believe in Him. He became a human being with the sole purpose of giving us His life, embracing us, and lifting us into God's heart. This was the principal and most important goal of Christmas. Everything happened for this: the stable, the manger, the visit of the shepherds, the singing of the angels, everything took place for this: He wanted to make us God's own children. God became a child so that he would make us children of God. We are now God's children the same way that Jesus Himself is the Son of God as a human being. We are carrying in us God's immortal life, that which St. John called "eternal life" and for which the language of theology uses the name "sanctifying grace." This reality must make us child-like, joyful, carefree. After all, nothing really bad can happen to us once we became God's

children. Can we accept wholeheartedly this great dignity? Perhaps we allow God to enter into our Sundays and the minutes of our prayers, but do we exclude Him from the activities of our daily lives? If we recognize and consent that we are God's children, the only thing we have to do is to allow God to be our Father every minute of our every day. If we wish to make each of our days into Christmas, we have to live every day the wonderful reality that we are children of God.

2. If we are children of God, from that fact follows that we are brothers and sisters to each other. That our fellow men and women are our brothers and sisters means also that we should see in each of them our great Brother, Jesus Christ. But do we recognize Jesus in every person who turns to us with his or her needs? In the events of the first Christmas, there was nothing glamorous. The citizens of Bethlehem looked at the Holy Family as homeless people, vagrants. If we want to make each of our days into Christmas, we have to learn to see Jesus in every needy person and accept him or her as our beloved sibling. Would you refuse to give shelter to the Holy Family if you knew who they are? We know that in every needy person, Jesus stands at the door of our hearts. When the Son of God took our humanity on Himself, He made every human need into His own, and He identified Himself with everyone in need. That is why He did not want to be born in a royal palace and in luxury: He

wanted to experience every pain of the plight of being human and the suffering of the human heart. In this way the Son of God is still here among us in every human need.

3. The third gift of Christmas is that the birth of Jesus transformed the entire material world into a divine reality. When the Son of God became man in the tiny body of the Baby of Bethlehem, he lifted all the elements of that body, and with it the entire material world, to the level of the divine. He lifted earth to heaven—or heaven came down on earth. After all, marvelous things took place: a virgin gave birth to a child, angels sang above the dirty stable cave, a bright star led the wise men to the manger, bringing royal gifts for the newborn Baby wrapped in swaddling clothes. Since the body of man was made out of dust, when God became man, he became united with the dust of the earth. So this union made the entire material world divine. To use the phrase of the great French Jesuit scholar, Teilhard de Chardin: since the Son of God has made human nature his own, every human being now lives in a "divine milieu." This is the beginning of the restoration of the original state of Paradise, the inauguration of the messianic age, the beginning of the state of universal peace even in the midst of so many wars and violence.

St. Francis of Assisi understood this. He preached to the birds and made a deal with a wolf. He called the sun his brother, the moon his sister, and his own body "brother donkey." Even death he recognized as his sister. With the birth of Jesus, a new age dawned on the world, and the whole material world became a sacramental reality. In the world's matter, in this "stuff" that surrounds us, God appears for men: this is what we see in the water of baptism, in the oil of confirmation, in the bread and wine of the Holy Eucharist. Our entire year becomes Christmas, as even the category of time is lifted up and becomes heavenly. If we consider the material world holy, as the very elements that made up the Body of Christ, we see all the elements as means by which God Himself comes among us and enters our lives. Every day will become Christmas, if instead of greed we could use this matter according to God's will, if instead of exploitation we could respect the harmony of nature, by discovering in the material world God's magnificent plans of salvation.

Let us keep this beautiful feast, one of the greatest days of the year a lasting reality in our lives. Let us make every day of the year a Christmas day.

11

THE HOLY FAMILY

The Sunday within the octave of Christmas reminds us that the Son of God, when He became man, did not want to live as a hermit but as a member of a warm, loving family, making His family a model for all families. The gospel readings of the three-year liturgical cycle are all episodes taken from the life of the Holy Family. In the *A year*, we have the story of the Holy Family's flight to Egypt; we read in the *B year* the passage which describes the presentation of the Baby Jesus in the Jerusalem Temple. In the *C year,* we hear the account of the event of the twelve-year-old Jesus remaining in the Temple of Jerusalem. All three events tell in one way or another about a crisis situation in the life of the Holy Family. In their flight to Egypt, the three members of the Holy Family became homeless refugees for years in a foreign land. In the story of the presentation in the Temple the future suffering of Jesus and Mary is predicted. Jesus' remaining in the Temple without the knowledge of His parents is seemingly the story of a teenage rebellion against one's parents. Family life in general is today in a crisis situation. The three gospel readings show us how to handle crises in our families. We can ask the question: in what way can the Holy Family be a model for a Christian family today?

Let's imagine a good Catholic family in today's world. Suppose that it's a large family—Mom and Dad have six children. When parents have a large family, it's not easy to provide food and clothing and everything else needed for a decent daily life. Don't you think that once in a while, in the middle of all the whirlwind of daily family life, the question would enter the minds of this Mom and Dad whether it's fair to set the family of Jesus, Mary, and Joseph as the model of all Christian families? After all, Joseph and Mary had only one child to raise, and daily life at their time was much simpler and much less expensive than today. How could their family life and ours be compared? How could today's families follow the example of the Holy Family in our complicated age? To answer such a question, I'd say that the Holy Family is our model not so much for the size of the family, or for their cultural or ethnic background, or for their social status or financial means. The family of Jesus, Mary, and Joseph is our model not for any of its visible features but for the soul, the spirit, the heart that animated that family.

Looking back to the second half of the 19th century, we can find a good example of someone trying to model his life on the life of the Holy Family. Blessed Charles de Foucauld was an officer of the French Foreign Legion from which he was dismissed because of his dissolute life. In 1886, at the age of 28, he went through a conversion experience; he converted to Christianity, and, since he wanted to be a Cistercian monk, he entered a Trappist monastery in France. Some time later, feeling the call and desire to follow Jesus' way of life more closely, he left the monastery, moved to the Holy Land, to Nazareth, the town where Jesus lived for thirty

Chapter 11: The Holy Family

years, and became a servant in a convent of Poor Clare nuns. He tried to imitate literally the life of the Holy Family. He thought that to imitate Jesus' life he had to live on the very spot where Jesus and His family lived. A few years later he realized that this was not necessary. He himself wrote down this thought in moving words: "This life of Nazareth was to be led elsewhere than in the Holy Land. This divine banquet whose minister I was to become [as a priest], had to be offered to the lame, blind, and poor, to people, that is, [who live] without priests. In Morocco, with ten million inhabitants, there was not a single priest...." He spent the rest of his life deep in the Sahara Desert in a small village among the miserably poor Tuareg tribe. His life was ended at the age of fifty-eight when robbers attacked the village and shot him to death.

Charles de Foucauld demonstrated by his very life that to follow the life of the Holy Family we have to imitate not the external circumstances but, rather, we have to make our own the inner attitude that motivated and moved Jesus and His parents. Then this inner attitude will be reflected and expressed; it will become visible and radiate in our daily lives. I'd sum up this inner attitude in three points that are closely connected with each other:

1. <u>Obedience to God's will,</u> which means obedience to God's personal call. This obedience manifests itself in big decisions that change one's entire life—like choosing a way of life, or choosing a profession, or choosing a spouse, or choosing religious and/or priestly life. This obedience should show itself also in following God's will every day, even in every hour, in the smallest details of our daily life,

in a constant search, asking ourselves, "What is God's will for me <u>now</u>, for this given hour or situation?" This search is implicitly present in our minds all the time whenever we try to do "the right thing." We can discover this search for God's will in the details of the life of the Holy Family. For example, Mary and Joseph followed exactly the prescribed rituals when the Child was born, having Jesus first circumcised on the eighth day after His birth and then presenting Him at the Temple forty days after His birth. This fundamental obedience should be the basic driving force in our daily lives, just as it was for Jesus for whom His "daily bread" was to do His Father's will. This obedience includes our sincere, deep-seated, whole-hearted (which means non-rebellious) acceptance of our life situation, whatever that may be, and, as a result, the faithful, dedicated doing of everything that we are supposed to do. Jesus, Joseph, and Mary knew what their part in Salvation History was, knew their parts in God's plans, said their *Yes* to it and carried it out faithfully, day after day. We should do the same.

2. <u>Simplicity.</u> The Holy Family lived a simple life in a simple home in a simple town. There was nothing glamorous about it. As a respected craftsman of the local community, Joseph ensured for Mary and Jesus a life without misery or destitution. Certainly, there was nothing fancy about their simple daily life as Jewish village-dwellers. What *was* special was their way of thinking about their daily life, about their earthly possessions. It was the attitude that we call

spiritual poverty. Spiritual poverty means that, independently of how much or how little wealth one has, the person is not attached to material goods. It means that material possessions are not the highest priority in his life; his life's main emphasis or main interest is not money or things. The person knows that material goods are necessary for daily life but he knows also that they are not so important; they are just the means in his life toward higher goals, not the goal itself. The ultimate purpose of our daily work should be simply helping other people and praising God by our various activities, not making as much money as possible.

3. The life of the Holy Family was a life of <u>acceptance of crosses</u> and preparation for crosses. We see this spirit of readiness to accept suffering in the story of Jesus' presentation in the Temple. It was a Jewish religious custom to present the first-born son and to offer him to God's service. As a sign of this presentation, the parents offered an animal sacrifice. Although in the case of every other first-born boy this offering was just symbolic, in the case of Jesus it became a reality. The Father accepted the offering and this acceptance was fulfilled in Christ's death on the Cross. The holocaust of the presentation of the Child was offered on Calvary Hill, on the Cross of Christ. This is why old Simeon prophesied that Jesus will be "contradicted": His words will be challenged and opposed, and He will have to

fight against resistance. At the same time, Simeon predicted that Mary's heart will be pierced by a sword. Jesus' whole education, his whole hidden life, and his public ministry were preparation for His death on the Cross, for a suffering in which Mary will also have a painful share.

Some time ago, I read this saying: "We don't know what the future holds for us but we know who holds the future." We don't know what this present year or present week or present day will bring but we know that whatever it will bring will come from God's loving hands; even the minor or major crosses and sufferings will serve His purpose and be for us a share in Christ's suffering. Let us be generous and ready to accept these tests and trials because we know that for those who love God, everything serves for their good (cf. Rom 8:28), even their sufferings. One day we will discover that our crosses were blessings in disguise. Just remember the vision of Emperor Constantine: on the eve of his decisive battle, in a vision, he saw the sign of the Cross in the sky with these words under it: *"In hoc signo vinces,--*In this sign you'll be victorious." The (up to that time) pagan Emperor then ordered his army to put the Cross and other Christian symbols on the top of all their flags, banners, and standards. He went on to win a decisive victory. The Battle of the Milvian Bridge took place between the Roman Emperors Constantine I and Maxentius on October 28, 312. This victory paved the way for Christianity to become a world religion. The Cross is our sign of triumph not because it defeated Christ on Calvary Hill but because by it Christ defeated death and sin and all the powers of evil.

This is the message of the Holy Family for us: Let's follow the example of the Holy Family by acquiring the same spirit that lived in them—the spirit of obedience, the spirit of spiritual poverty, and the spirit of readiness to accept our crosses.

12

THE DIVINE MOTHERHOOD OF MARY

Back in 1960, during my seminary years in Rome, I visited with a group the headquarters of an apostolic movement, the *Centro Per Un Mondo Migliore* or *Center for a Better World*, at Rocca di Papa in the vicinity of the Eternal City. In one of the several chapels of the institution, I was fascinated by a painting of the event of Annunciation. I've never seen an image of the young girl Mary as beautiful and radiant as in that picture. Our tour guide told us that the title of the painting is *Our Lady of Yes*, and explained that the painter wanted to catch in his painting the very moment when Mary pronounces her *Yes* to God's invitation to become the Mother of God's Son. The artwork expresses perfectly the prompt readiness of the young Virgin Mary. I could never forget the expression of willingness shining on Mary's face.

Christ was conceived only once, right? Right. Christ was born only once, right? Right. He died only once and rose from the dead only once, right? Right again. Yet, we celebrate these events every year. The annual celebration of the events of Christ's life does not mean that they would be repeated, taking place again and again every day. Yet, in the liturgical celebration we not just remember past events. It's true, they are historical events, each happening only once in the past. They took place only once, but by their annual celebration, these same historical events, in the Church's liturgy they mysteriously become present, the congregation re-live the one event again in mystery. Each Christian feast's annual celebration is a *kairos* a grace-filled time of salvation, a special, extraordinary moment, eternity itself breaking into the chronological time.

The purpose of this short introduction is to make the point that other ancient religions, most of them containing myths of many gods, follow a cycle, go around in a circle, year after year, and their myths are happening all over again innumerable times. In contrast to these religions, the Judeo-Christian faith follows a straight line, a chronological progression of historical events, beginning with the creation of the universe, advancing centuries after centuries through the patriarchs, prophets, and kings, toward the "fullness of time," the time of Incarnation when the Son of God was born from a Virgin as a man in Jesus of Nazareth. This salvation history still continues toward a final end, the Parousia, the second coming of Jesus, following God's eternal plan of salvation. Of this salvation history we people living in the 21st century are also an integral part. There is a definite direction, a constant progression and moving forward manifested in history. We should see also the events of the Birth of Christ in this context and not just as isolated incidents. The Conception and Birth of Christ were the greatest events in mankind's history since Creation; they were the fulfillment of all of God's promises made for hundreds of years to the Jewish people who were chosen by God to prepare for the coming of the Messiah.

Chapter 12: The Divine Motherhood of Mary

At the dawn of the creation of human beings, something went wrong, terribly wrong. God had created the human being not just "good" as all other parts of creation but, as the book of Genesis says, "very good," better than all the other material beings combined, better than all the galaxies, oceans, mountains, forests, and animals. Man and woman were created in the very image and likeness of God as free and intelligent beings who had a soul that would never die but would be immortal, beings who even share God's inner eternal life within the Holy Trinity. But, unfortunately, this special gift, their freedom got the human beings into trouble: they rebelled against their Creator, they wanted to be their own god. By this act of disobedience Evil entered the world, corrupting the entire beautiful creation of God. Pain and hard work became part of human life, and man and woman, though originally even their bodies were created for immortality, had to suffer in many different ways and, ultimately, had to die.

We know that God's plan of salvation was badly frustrated by Adam and Eve's disobedience when they rebelled against God and tried to become their own god. But God's plan was unfolding even in the darkest hour after the original sin. Immediately after the first couple's rebellion, God said to Satan, the evil spirit, the serpent who tempted and seduced man and woman: "I'll put enmity between you and the woman, and between your offspring and hers; he'll strike at your head while you strike at his heel." Who is this mysterious woman? Yes, this statement meant that there will be a woman whose offspring will crush the serpent's head. This first promise of reparation was repeated many times through the following centuries so that as new generations of people were born, they would not forget it. One of these repeated promises we read in Isaiah: "The Lord himself will give you this sign: the virgin shall be with child, and bear a son, and shall name him Immanuel" (Is 7:14). As the long period of expectation and preparation approached its end and the time of the fulfillment of the promises was close, a woman (the Christian tradition calls her Anna) conceived a baby girl, the only one in the entire humankind without the original sin, without that sad heritage left on their descendants by the first parents of the human race. This baby girl, Mary, anticipated and signaled the things to come: the return of innocence, the restoration of the sanctifying grace to mankind (men and women being not only creatures of God but also His very own children, by sharing God's divine life of the Holy Trinity), and even immortality of body.

When that baby girl, Mary, was conceived and born without the stain of original sin (we call this mystery the Immaculate Conception), God's ancient promise was near to its fulfillment: mankind's salvation was being unfolded, and in the person of Mary the prototype of the redeemed humanity appeared on earth, anticipating the redemption worked out by the death and resurrection of her Son, Jesus Christ. When Mary was born, in her person the new Temple arrived, the Temple that would house the great God of glory, Jesus Christ. When Mary was born, the future mother of the Savior arrived, but the divine Craftsman would work on her. He would make her gradually even more beautiful, would adorn her through the years of preparation with the best of virtues to become the person who would say an unequivocal *Yes* to God's offer to

Chapter 12: The Divine Motherhood of Mary

become the mother of the Savior of humankind. She would become a person of absolute acceptance and receptivity, a person who would show not even in the least way any resistance to God's knocking on her door, who by her *Yes* response would completely make up for Eve's rebellion and disobedience and thus would reverse the name "Eva" into the *"Ave"* of the angel Gabriel: *"Ave Maria,* ... Hail Mary." We're eye-witnesses here: we see God's plan unfolding, becoming reality in the most beautiful way. We see in the person of Mary God's masterpiece: a human being reaching her perfection.

Mary is not just one of the many saints, not even just the greatest of all the saints: She has a unique, irreplaceable role in mankind's history. She is the Mother of God's own Son, of the second Person of the Holy Trinity, and thus Mary herself is called the Mother of God, *Theotokos,* God-bearer. There are millions of saints in heaven, but there is only one Mother of God, Mary. From among the billions of human persons born on earth through mankind's history, only one human being was chosen for this tremendous distinction. The mother of the king is herself a queen, and so Mary, Mother of Christ the King, ruler of the universe, became the Queen of Heaven and Earth. What a unique place, what an unfathomable dignity for a mere human being! Can we ever comprehend what it means to give birth to God as a newborn Baby? To nurse Him, to fondle Him, to teach Him to speak, to cook for Him, to wash His clothes, to see Him growing up in the home?

But she is even more! The Son of God, Jesus Christ, by taking up and making His own our human body and soul, our human nature, became a brother of all human beings. By dying for us on the Cross and rising from the dead, He liberated us from the guilt of our sins, and by that act He made us God's children again. If Christ made us His brothers and sisters, He made His own mother also <u>our</u> mother. All the saints are our brothers and sisters but a heavenly mother we have only one: the Blessed Virgin Mary, mother of Jesus Christ.

Then we look at ourselves: we're the almost finished products of God's redeeming activity. Yes, in baptism we received the same innocence and beauty that Mary possessed even without baptism; and all the more we should feel ashamed and repentant that we were not able to preserve this innocence. That we did not say always "Yes" to God's many calls, that we resisted His graces so many times by our laziness or conceitedness or hatred—in any case, by the hardness of our hearts—we closed the door before God and before our brothers and sisters. We rebelled against God's will and command. Looking alternately at Mary and at ourselves and seeing who she is and what we are, the beauty that she is and the mess we made of ourselves, we must be filled with tremendous sorrow. Sorrow and even anger at ourselves for being so stubborn and stupid to squander God's precious graces. But at the same time we are also filled with hope. Mary is a mother, not only Jesus' mother but also our mother, who sees us covered with dirt and ugliness, and looks at us as her children. She leads us to her Son, who washes away the ugliness of our sins with His own blood. After our sins are forgiven and forgotten, we regain our beauty and innocence that befits us as the brothers and sisters of Jesus and children of His Mother, Mary.

Chapter 12: The Divine Motherhood of Mary

As a fitting conclusion, let's listen to the words of Archbishop Fulton Sheen: "There is, actually, only one person in all humanity of whom God has one picture and in whom there is a perfect conformity between what He wanted her to be and what she is, and that is His own mother. Most of us are a minus sign, in the sense that we do not fulfill the high hopes the heavenly Father has for us. But Mary is the equal sign. The ideal that God had of her, equals with what she is in the flesh. The model and the copy are perfect; she is all that was foreseen, planned, and dreamed. The melody of her life is played just as it was written."

13

EPIPHANY

Sometimes we may wonder: Why on earth do we celebrate the Birth of Jesus twice every year? Why do we have two birthdays of Christ, at Christmas and at Epiphany? The short answer to these questions is that one of the two feasts is to hide Christ's glory, and the other feast day is to reveal it. Christmas Day is to hide Jesus' divinity in the simple story of the birth of Jesus in Bethlehem as a simple human Baby; the second feast, Epiphany, is to reveal the true never-heard-before glory of the unpretentious beginning of the life of this Child.

Once in a while, we can witness a solar eclipse over the United States when the Moon covers the Sun. I remember, a few years ago in some parts of the United States, the Sun was completely covered by the Moon, while we, here in Texas saw a partial, yet nearly total eclipse: just a little crescent of the Sun was visible. At that time, we were seriously warned that trying to look at the Sun with the naked eye could blind us. The Sun's brilliance is just too much for the human eyes, so only through very dark glasses could we safely watch the eclipse. The Sun had to become almost completely hidden to be made visible for the human eyes. In other words, the "revelation" or showing of the Sun could take place only by hiding it. Revelation by hiding.

The case is exactly the same with God. When God wanted to come among us human beings, He had to hide his glory. God's glory is infinitely bright. In the Old Testament we read that God is a consuming fire, and whoever would see God would die. Our weak humanity cannot bear the brilliant glory of God. That's why when God decided to come among us, He had to hide the brilliance of His divinity and come to us as a human being. Even as a human being He was born as a tiny, weak, newborn infant. He did not want to frighten man: He wanted man to love Him, and who would not love a helpless infant? This is the reason why the Son of God, the Second Person of the Holy Trinity, chose to be born as a Baby. And even as a Baby, He was not born in wealth and power but in utter simplicity, to an unknown (but holy, immaculate) woman. The birth had to take place in utter poverty, outside the city of Bethlehem. So He was to be born as the child of a homeless couple, in a cave that was used as a stable. He was laid on hay in a manger, warmed by the bodies of domestic animals, and first visited by simple, dirty, uneducated shepherds. No glamor, just simplicity and poverty. "The Word was made flesh and dwelt among us" in a completely hidden manner.

Rather than <u>hiding</u> the divinity of the Son of God in poverty, the Epiphany is the <u>revealing</u> of God among us. The word "revelation" means "removing the veil;" what was veiled so far, is now revealed. The word "epiphany" means showing, manifestation. At Epiphany we celebrate the revelation (removal of the veil) or manifestation of the divinity of this Child of Bethlehem. Of course, the revelation is partial, just like a partial eclipse. We could not tolerate a total revelation; we would be not just blinded but burnt to ashes.

Chapter 13: Epiphany

On the feast of Epiphany, we celebrate God's revelation among us not just in one but in three gospel episodes.

The first episode is the visit of the Wise Men at the manger of Jesus. The Wise Men are not Jewish: they are from far-away countries, not of the Old Testament people. They are pagans, or, as the Jews would call them, Gentiles. They represent the non-Jewish nations. They learned about the new King by a cosmic event: a strange star appears on the sky. It seems the Wise Men were astrologers whose job was to study the nocturnal skies. The star reveals the new King; the cosmos, God's inanimate created world, also participates in revealing the arrival of the Emmanuel, the God-with-us, the mystery of Incarnation. The astrologers obey the heavenly sign: from faraway Orient, they come, following the star to the newborn King, bringing Him precious gifts of gold, frankincense, and myrrh—gold for the King, frankincense for God, and myrrh for His burial. The Wise Men, by revealing the glory of Jesus, the God-man, are prophets sent both for the Jews and for the Nations (Gentiles). Their visit and worship at Jesus' crib is an invitation for us to do the same.

The second gospel episode of revealing this hidden God among us is the Baptism of Jesus in the Jordan River. When Jesus came to be baptized by John the Baptist, John introduced Jesus to the Jewish crowd who had been waiting to be baptized as the Lamb of God who will take away the sins of the world. After John reluctantly baptized Jesus, the skies opened and the mystery of Holy Trinity was announced to the world for the first time. As Jesus rose from the water, the Holy Spirit hovered above His head in the form of a dove, and the Father's voice sounded saying, "This is my beloved Son, with whom I am well pleased" (Mt 3:17). This was revelation not only for the crowd that happened to be present but for every man and woman on earth. It is the first revelation that the one God is not a solitary Person in an icy loneliness but a community, a family of three Persons, Father, Son, and Holy Spirit. Jesus is the Word made flesh, the Son, the Second Person of the Holy Trinity who reveals the Father to the human family. The Son is the Father's revelation (hiding and unveiling at the same time, revealing by hiding) to every human being, to you and me. In the words of St. John the Evangelist, "God is Love". God could not be love if He were alone: love is possible only in a community. This mystery was revealed at the Baptism of Jesus.

The third gospel episode of revealing God by hiding is Jesus' first miracle at the wedding at Cana when He changed a huge amount of water into vintage wine at the request of His mother. By this miracle Jesus openly stated that with His coming a new age dawned on the earth, that the Old Testament ended and the New Testament began; the plain water signified the Old Testament and the sweet, intoxicating wine the New Testament. It is also important to notice that this first miracle happened at a wedding: Jesus came to establish the marriage between heaven and earth, God and man, just as it was before the original sin. At the creation of man, God created man and woman in His image and likeness and gave them a share in God's own divine life, so that they could participate in the eternal flow of love between Father, Son, and Holy Spirit. What a glorious plan! Unfortunately, by the original sin of disobedience this connection between God and the human race was tragically broken and humankind lived under the dark sky of infinite distance from God. But God did not reject men and women forever. He made a plan to reconnect humankind with heaven, and this re-connection happened first by God becoming man, Jesus of Nazareth, the obedient new Adam, and, as a second step, by the death of the Son of God on the cross followed by His glorious resurrection. By Jesus' death and resurrection all the sins of humankind were expiated, and, at His ascension, Jesus took His glorified human body as the first fruit of the whole human race into heaven. At Cana, Jesus called His mother "the Woman," indicating that this mystical wedding between Jesus Christ and humankind will take place through and in the Mother Church of which Mary, Mother of God, is the model and its first representative. In the gospel of John Mary is called "the Woman" again by Jesus on Calvary Hill, as she stood under the cross of the dying Jesus in the company of the Apostle John. In a moving scene, Jesus, hanging on the cross, close to death, entrusts His mother into the care of John, and gives John to Mary as her Son. Under the cross, the Apostle John represents all of us human beings. Thus, this solemn act of Christ makes Mary the mother of us all. It is a call that we should love our heavenly Mother tenderly and trustingly.

By these brief reflections we may be able to realize how fitting it is to celebrate the birth of Christ not by one but by two solemnities, Christmas and Epiphany. The two feasts together express the greatness and the depth of the mystery of Incarnation. We understand with humble devotion that the birth of the Christ-child is, at the same time, a hiding of the blinding brilliance of God's greatness and the revealing of God's coming to us in the Baby of Bethlehem. By His plan, the brilliance of His coming would neither kill us nor blind us but would make us able to fathom God's infinite, invincible love for each of us human beings.

14

BAPTISM OF JESUS

On Sunday during the third week after Christmas, as a final closing of the Christmas Season, the Church celebrates Jesus' baptism in the Jordan River at the beginning of His public ministry. Of course, Jesus' baptism was not the same as the sacrament of baptism in the Catholic Church. Jesus was baptized by the baptism of John the Baptist, which was only a simple penitential rite, an expression of sorrow for sins. Of course, Jesus did not need to express sorrow for sins: He was the all-holy Son of God. His taking share in John the Baptist's baptism was to show His absolute solidarity with every human being, with every sinner. As Jesus was standing in line waiting to be baptized, John noticed Him. He pointed at Jesus, saying, "Behold, the Lamb of God, who takes away the sin of the world" (John 1:29). Understandably, John protested when Jesus asked him for baptism, but Jesus insisted: It has to be done. It had to be done because beyond the expression of Jesus' humility and His union with the human race, it was the solemn inauguration of Jesus' public ministry, the commencement of the messianic times, and the fulfillment of all of God's promises of salvation, prophesized by ancient prophets for countless centuries.

Jesus' baptism was also the occasion when the greatest of all the great mysteries, the mystery of the Holy Trinity, was revealed to humankind. After the only begotten Son of God was baptized, the skies opened, and the Father's voice came from heaven, saying, "This is my beloved Son, with whom I am well pleased" (Mt 3:17), and the Holy Spirit was hovering above Jesus' head in the form of a dove. Through this revelation, human beings could learn that God is not a solitary Being existing in an icy loneliness but a loving divine family of three Persons, Father, Son, and Holy Spirit.

Ancient Christian authors point out also that when Jesus was baptized, it was not the waters that would make Jesus holy: As the Son of God, He has been the Holy One for all eternity. What happened was rather that the waters were made holy by touching Jesus' body so that from that time onward the waters received the ability to make holy everyone who receives the sacrament of baptism. Jesus' baptism gave rise to the first and most important one of the sacraments by which a human being was able to enter God's world, become a member of the Church, and share in the eternal inner life of the Holy Trinity. Jesus' baptism, by the baptism of John the Baptist, was the transition from John's baptism of repentance to Jesus' baptism of new life.

What happens when someone (an adult or a baby) is baptized by Jesus' baptism? Baptism is a life-changing experience, not just some nice little ritual after a baby has been born. Maybe the power of baptism can be illustrated by a story.

Thor Heyerdahl was a great sea adventurer. He became famous for his _Kon-Tiki_ expedition in 1947, in which he sailed 8,000 km (5,000 miles) across the South Pacific Ocean, from South America to the Tuamotu Islands, in a simple, hand-built raft. The expedition was designed to demonstrate that ancient people could have made long sea voyages, creating contacts between apparently separate cultures.

Few people knew that this famous sea voyager once had a deathly fear of water. But something happened to change all that. During WW II, Thor trained in Canada with the Free Norwegian Forces. One day he was canoeing down a dangerous river. The river ended in a waterfall. Suddenly the canoe capsized plunging Thor into the raging river. As the swirling water swept him helplessly toward the waterfall, a strange thought entered his mind. It occurred to him that he would soon learn which of his parents was right about life after death. His father believed that there was such life, his mother did not.

Then another strange thing happened. The words of the Lord's Prayer popped into his head, and he began to pray. A burst of energy began to surge through his body. Thor began to battle the river. Some mysterious force was helping him. A few minutes later he reached shore.

The Thor Heyerdahl who climbed out of the river was totally different from the one who was plunged into the river. The waters of the river had "baptized" him, so to speak, into a new life. First of all, the old Heyerdahl had a deathly fear of water. The new Heyerdahl did not. Second, the old Heyerdahl had questions about God and life after death. The new Heyerdahl did not.

Heyerdahl's experience in the waters of the river is a beautiful illustration of what happens to us in the waters of baptism. The person we are after baptism is totally different from the person we were before baptism. Before baptism, we were physically alive but without the divine life. God implanted this divine life in the first human couple, Adam and Eve, but they lost it by their conceitedness by which they wanted to be their own god. God decided to give back this life to human beings: for this purpose, He sent us His Son as the man Jesus Christ. The way to regain this divine life is to believe in Jesus and to receive baptism. After baptism, we are spiritually alive in Christ. We are a totally new person, living a totally new life, God's own Trinitarian life.

Every human being is a child of our first parents, Adam and Eve, who were created beautiful, happy, and holy. They were perfect human beings but, beyond that, they received the special gift of sharing in God's eternal life. But they were tested and, unfortunately, they failed the test. As a result, they were expelled from that state of happiness which is called Paradise or Eden. They lost God's friendship and, because of that, they lost also the gift of sharing God's own life. From that time on, something important was missing from their existence. This absence of God's life (which is called also sanctifying grace) is what we call original sin. Thus, we have to understand correctly what original sin means. It's not something "bad" added to the person's life, like some dirty spots on a white gown. The original sin is an absence, something important missing, and this something is the sanctifying grace, God's divine life, the tremendous gift by which God wants to enrich every human being.

God promised that one day this gift or grace will be returned to man. This promise was fulfilled only after a long time, after several thousands of years, when Jesus was born. Jesus was the New Adam (His mother, Mary, being the New Eve), the firstborn of the new humanity. Like the first Adam, this New Adam was also tested by his suffering and death on the cross, but He was found obedient. By His obedience, up to the point of dying on the cross, He regained for the human race the gift that the first Adam lost by his disobedience. He regained God's friendship for every human being, offered as a free gift to everyone who was ready to accept it. By the coming of Jesus, by His life and teaching, by His suffering, death, and resurrection, man received the power to become God's friend again and to share again in his soul God's creative power and life. This receiving back God's friendship and life takes place in the sacrament of baptism.

The baby receives his or her natural life, the fullness of humanity, from the parents: This is the first birth of the child, a perfect human being. But something is still missing: the gift of God's life. The baby has to be born not only from the human mother but also from Mother Church at the fountain of baptism. Baptism is the second birth of the child. After baptism, he or she is God's beloved child, made in His own image and likeness, endowed with God's eternal life. This means that we Christians carry two lives in ourselves: the natural life which we received from our parents, and the supernatural life, God's own life, that we receive in baptism and which is increased and strengthened each time when we receive Communion.

The image of an electric appliance may illustrate the power that baptism provides for us. The lamp, as long as it is not plugged in, cannot shed light. After it is plugged into the electric current, energy flows through it and the lamp gives bright light. Any other electric appliance, like a computer or a vacuum cleaner or a washing machine, will function according to the purpose for which it was produced—as long as it is plugged in. Baptism adds the divine power to our mere humanity which makes man able to achieve fantastic feats.

This new life that a person receives through baptism may not remain stagnant: it has to grow. Just as a farmer grafts a twig from one tree to another tree, so baptism grafts us to the Body of Christ. Baptism is not the end of a process: It's the beginning; it's merely the first step. Once a twig is grafted to a tree branch, it needs to grow and become part of the tree. If it doesn't, it will soon die. The same is true of baptism. Once we are grafted to Christ, we must grow and become part of Him. If we don't, we will die.

But how do we do this? How does this growth take place? How do we grow and become part of Christ? St. Paul gives us the answer: "As you received Christ Jesus the Lord, walk in him, rooted in him and built upon him and established in the faith. … Put on compassion, kindness, humility, gentleness, and patience, bearing with one another and forgiving one another. And over all these put on love" (Col 2:6-7; 3:12-14).

In other words, we grow and become part of Christ by imitating Christ into whose body we have been grafted by baptism. We treat others kindly as Christ has treated us. We treat others patiently as Christ has treated us. We forgive others as Christ has forgiven us. We love others as Christ has loved us. In short, we grow and become part of Christ by imitating Christ, whose life we received in baptism.

15

PRESENTATION

The Christmas cycle of the Christian liturgical year closes on February 2, the feast of the Presentation of the Lord in the Jerusalem Temple, forty days after Christmas. Let's meditate briefly on this episode of the Lord's life.

Jesus and His family, soon after the Child's birth in Bethlehem, had to go through three Jewish religious ceremonies. First, on the eighth day after his birth, every male child had to be circumcised by the rabbi at the local synagogue. By this ceremony, the child became incorporated into the Covenant that bound the Hebrew nation in a love union with God. That little cut on the sex organ of the child made him able, when grown up and married, to engender new children of the Covenant.

Second, after giving birth to a child, every mother had to go through a purification service. In the case of the birth of a girl, this took place on the eighth day after birth; in the case of the birth of a boy, the service was held forty days after the birth. At this time, she had to bring to the Temple a lamb for a burnt sacrifice (holocaust) and a pigeon for a sin offering. For poor families it was allowed that instead of an expensive lamb they could bring two pigeons. The offering of two pigeons instead of a lamb and a pigeon was called the "Offering of the Poor." That Mary and Joseph brought in the Temple two pigeons indicated their social status: they belonged to the poorer social class.

Third, after the birth of the firstborn son, the boy was considered sacred to God, belonging exclusively to God. This way of looking at a firstborn son originated from the attitude of appreciation of and gratefulness for the gift of new life. But, in a negative way, it may have been the relic of the custom of pagan tribes which offered their firstborn son to their gods as a burnt sacrifice. For the Israelites, the ceremony of the presentation of the child in the Temple was called the "Redemption of the Firstborn," by which, in a symbolic way, the son was "bought back" from God by a monetary offering. The sum of five shekels had to be paid to the priest. This could not be done sooner than thirty-one days after the birth but had to be done without much delay after that.

All three of these ceremonies may sound strange in our ears today, but in the context of the Israelite life they all expressed the awareness that the child is a gift of God. Of all of God's gifts the greatest is (and puts the greatest responsibility on the shoulders of the parents) the gift of a child.

As we can see, the Holy Family's celebration forty days after Jesus' birth was actually a double celebration: that of the Purification ceremony and that of the Presentation of the Child in the Temple. Before Vatican II the feast was called the Purification; now it is called the Presentation of the Lord. Putting the emphasis on the Presentation aspect of the day emphasizes it as a feast of the Lord rather than a Marian feast. As a devout Jewish family, Mary and Joseph took the Baby Jesus forty days after His birth into the

Jerusalem Temple to satisfy the prescriptions of the Law and to present the firstborn Child and dedicate Him to the service of God. In the case of Jesus, this was not only a symbolic act. While in the case of other male babies, the boy was given back to the parents, Jesus was given totally, 100%, to God; He became the person for whom His daily bread was to fulfill the will of God, His Father. He was not "bought back" by some monetary contribution or animal sacrifice.

The full meaning of this religious act was illustrated by two elderly persons, a man, Simeon, and a woman, Anna. Both were present in the Temple at that particular hour as they both were waiting for the redemption of Israel. As two old persons, they represented the Old Testament, the old people of God, the chosen nation who were waiting for centuries for the arrival of the Messiah. As members of both genders, Simeon and Anna also represented every human being, the entire human race, which was now, at the fullness of time, ready to receive the world's Savior. Simeon even got the privilege to hold the Child in his arms. We repeat this privilege when on this day we carry a burning candle in our hands in a procession. The candle represents the Christ Child; hence, the old English name of the feast is Candlemas.

Simeon's prophetic words further explain the significance of the momentous event. He declares that he is ready to die now because, after the waiting of many years, he finally was able to see the arrival of the Redeemer, "a light for revelation to the Gentiles, and the glory of your people Israel" (Luke 2:32). He tells Mary, the Child's mother, "Behold, this Child is destined for the fall and rise of many in Israel" (Luke 2:34). Christ will be the key person in history: Every person's relationship to Him will decide his or her eternal destiny. Simeon also says that Mary's own heart will be pierced by a sword, that she will participate in the sufferings of her Son. The coming of this Child is "the sign of contradiction," the decisive event by which everyone will be judged: Those who will believe in Him and follow Him will rise to eternal life, and those who will reject Him will fall from the grace of God forever. Before this Child everyone has to make a decision for or against, and this decision will define the person's destiny—whether he or she will find meaning and happiness in life, or see the world and the events of his or her life as meaningless and absurd.

The feast of the Lord's Presentation is a call to each of us to renew our unconditional *Yes* to Jesus Christ who is the final answer to all the great questions of our lives, the *Yes* or *Fiat* response that we made at Baptism and repeat at our Confirmation.

16

VALENTINE'S DAY

During the first half of February as Valentine's Day is approaching, we experience its closeness wherever we go: shopping malls and stores are decorated with an infinite number of heart-shaped figures in different shades of red, flower shops are jammed with red roses, grocery stores have big displays of heart-shaped boxes of chocolates, and each home gets scores of pretty Valentine cards. What do these millions of hearts around us tell us? They tell something about the importance of love and friendship in our lives. They tell us in an unequivocal way that what ultimately keeps the world running is not the great scientific or technological inventions, nor the wisdom of politicians and world leaders, nor the immutable rules of the world economy, but the simple fact that people care for each other, that the bond of love is an inestimably strong tie among them, that people are ready to work and make great sacrifices for their families and friends. They tell us that people like nurses and doctors, priests, ministers and teachers, police officers and firemen dedicate selflessly their time, energy, education, and even their lives to people entrusted to their care. They do this not only to make a living but because they want to help their fellowmen and women, because they are important to them.

But even the million hearts of Valentine's Day cannot make us forget the millions of broken hearts, the millions of broken marriages and broken friendships, because we're reminded daily of the fleeting character of human love, because we're living in a broken world. So, the million hearts of Valentine's Day tell more about our <u>hunger</u> for love than about its reality. We hunger constantly after a love that is lasting, that overcomes all obstacles, bridges all abysses, surmounts all distances. We hunger for a reality in which every friend, every lover not only promises but also keeps the promise, "I will love you forever." Every love carries with itself the promise to last forever, and we realize with bitterness how fleeting and short-lived most loves are.

Is there such a thing as Eternal Love at all or does it exist only in our dreams? Yes, there <u>does exist</u> an Eternal Love; there <u>is</u> one. Yes, there is one, but only one, yet that one is enough. This one Eternal Love dwells in the heart of the One in whom the whole of eternity is present, in the heart of the man who came from Nazareth and, out of love, died on the cross; it dwells in the heart of the man whose name is Jesus of Nazareth. That heart, pierced by a soldier's lance, pierced by our sins, is the image, the icon, and, at the same time, the dwelling place of God's Eternal Love. So, the million hearts of Valentine's Day ultimately point toward one heart, the pierced and risen heart of Jesus.

When the apostle Saint John in his letter wanted to give us a brief definition of who God is, he put it in three short words: "God is love" (1 John 4:8). We can imagine God as a huge heart throbbing with an eternal, unlimited love. Before anything was created,

Chapter 16: Valentine's Day

there existed nothing else but the tremendous, eternal flow of infinite love between the Father, Son, and Holy Spirit. Then, inspired and urged by this love, God created the universe, and ever since His love supports and keeps in existence this created world. And it was out of this same love that He created each one of us. This tremendous love of God accompanies us always, wherever we go. We all are loved by an unquenchable Eternal Love.

True love tends to become similar to the object of its love. And so, God so loved the world, this struggling, hoping, stumbling humankind, that, at a certain point in history, He sent us His only Son to become a human being like us. He inserted His eternal Word, the message of His love into a human person, the person of Jesus Christ, so that He could speak to us in human words, and He put His immense divine love into one human heart, into the heart of Jesus. Yes, *all* of God's Eternal Love is dwelling in the heart of the man called Jesus of Nazareth. It happened the first time in the existence of the human race that a human being's heart was beating in synchrony with God's heart because Jesus' only wish was to do always the will of His Father. The purpose of His coming to us as a man was to make all human hearts similar to His own, to make them beat in synchrony with God's heart.

Nowadays many clocks and watches are electronically controlled so that they show the time to the second in synchrony with the atomic clock that is located in Denver, Colorado. Something like that is what Jesus wanted to achieve with our human hearts.

People like to brag about the advances of today's computer technology. They are proud that more and more memory can be stored in ever smaller computer chips, tiny down to microscopic level. This miniaturization is indeed impressive, but it is nothing in comparison to the condensation of God's Eternal Love into one single human heart, in the heart of Jesus. We are loved by God through the human heart of Jesus. The fullness of God's love, the totality of the stream of divine love cascading from the Holy Trinity, the love by which the universe was called into existence and has been kept in existence, God's unfathomable love toward each human being is hidden in the heart of Jesus.

Yes, there is in the world an Eternal Love, but only one, and that one Eternal Love resides in the heart of Jesus. And since this human heart of Jesus is the depository of God's unlimited love, it is, at the same time, the source of all true love that exists in the world, the love people have for one other. Eternal Love emanates, flows from the human heart of Jesus into millions of human hearts so that they can beat in sync with God's heart. Saint John says in his letter not only that God is love, but he adds that everyone who loves with an authentic love dwells in God and God dwells in him (cf. 1 John 4:16). It's true that here on earth what some people call "love," so many times is just a distorted caricature of the love God meant for us and it would be more correct to name it something else or to spell it "luv." That is because every true love is divine, its origin is God, and it comes from the human heart of Jesus. This true love is not a fleeting emotion but a tough, active, energetic love, a love that serves others humbly and faithfully, a love that keeps friends and families together, a love that makes the world turn.

The heart of the one Eternal Love, the heart of Jesus, can make our human loves long-lasting and permanent; it can make them such that they would endure through trials and crises, through long illnesses and long separations. The heart of Jesus can give our hearts the capability to become faithful hearts and can give them the strength and stability and vitality to be everlasting in friendship, in marriage, and in the celibate state when one gives his or her undivided love to Jesus, the divine Bridegroom.

We can say that the human heart of Jesus is the true center of the created universe; it is that atomic clock that wishes to control all human hearts. The totality of God's love is condensed into it, and all true love flows, pours, cascades from it into us. That's where we have to go – into Christ's heart – if we wish that our human love may have some likeness to the one Eternal Love. That's where we have to go to draw for our poor human love some permanence, some true warmth, some authenticity. May we have the courage and stamina to allow this divine fire to enter our little lives and set them ablaze with unquenchable, genuine love.

17

LENT

1. Just as the calendar of the Christian year is the result or the fruit of a development over several centuries, the season of Lent itself grew gradually into the liturgical interval as we know today. According to documentation from the second century, Christians held a strict fast from Holy Thursday through Easter morning, about forty hours from the time of the arrest of Jesus until His resurrection. They remembered Jesus' words: "The time will come when they will take away the bridegroom, and then they will fast" (Lk 5:35). At that time the motivation for fasting was the desire to share in the sufferings and death of Jesus. It was the <u>celebration</u> of the Paschal Mystery itself, not just a preparation for it.

    As the documents of the Council of Nicaea (325 AD) and the writings of several Church Fathers demonstrate, by the fourth century there was a six-week period of fasting observed as preparation for Easter. With this period Christians wanted to share in the forty-days-long fasting of Jesus. Since in the Christian tradition Sundays never counted as days of fast, the six times six days gave only thirty-six days, so later four more days were added at the beginning of Lent.

2. About the same time, in the patristic literature the <u>theology</u> of the holy seasons was also being continuously enriched. According to the teachings of the Church Fathers, the celebration of the events of Jesus' earthly life was more than the simple remembrance of the Lord's redeeming deeds. Through His Incarnation, the Son of God sanctified every earthly reality, including time. When the eternal Word of the Father entered creation, eternity itself broke into the category of time, and therefore Christians, friends of Jesus, living in the passing time but being connected with the eternal Word, touch eternity and, through grace, in a certain sense, they already possess it. For Jesus, every created reality, including the category of time, becomes a means by which He establishes connection with His followers. Through the liturgical celebration of the different events of Jesus' life, each particular event becomes a <u>present</u> reality and an opportunity for grace in the life of the Church and in the soul of the individual person. For this reason, the early Christian authors called the liturgical periods and solemnities *mysterium,* or *sacramentum.* They said, that through the perceptible earthly reality of time, God transmits supernatural grace for those who celebrate in faith this *mysterium* (a given event of Jesus' life). In the liturgical feast, in a way, the past becomes present: the past event takes place again, is happening again in mystery, and the

Christian community and the individual person re-live that particular event of Jesus' life. At Christmas Jesus is born, at Easter He is risen, at Pentecost Jesus comes to us in the Holy Spirit, and during Lent--as we pray more, fast, and keep vigil--Jesus shares with us His forty-day sojourn in the desert. Jesus wants to be with us. It depends on us, on the depth and sincerity of our devotion, whether or not we allow Him to enter our life, so that by His presence, He would sanctify our Lent.

3. The Latin name of Lent is *Quadragesima*, meaning "forty", and in all languages of Latin origin the name is connected with the number forty. What is the reason, that the length of Lent is forty days, not less, not more? Forty seems to be a special number in the Bible. As a matter of fact, in our biblical memories a whole series of events is connected with this number. Why?

In one of the first chapters of Genesis we read the story of the great flood. It was raining for forty days and forty nights while Noah and his family lived in the protection of the ark. This is not simple mathematics. The number is a sign: it calls our attention to an important reality. What is this reality?

Moses spends two times forty days and forty nights on the top of Mount Sinai. We have to see these two mountain sojourns in the right perspective. Do they have any connection with the great flood?

When the persecuted prophet Elijah goes to Mount Sinai to encounter God and to recover his vocation, his wanderings take forty days. Does the number forty come up again just by accident?

When the prophet Jonah preaches penance in the city of Nineveh, the time of waiting God gives for conversion is again forty days. Why forty? Why not more or less?

And when the Bible speaks not of one person but a whole nation, the people of God, the forty days become forty years that this people spends in the desert. Is it not surprising that the same number pops up again?

At the beginning of His public ministry, Jesus went to Jordan to be baptized by John. Following this solemn inauguration of his redemptive work, what is the first act the Holy Spirit prompted Him to do? He goes into the desert and keeps a fast of forty days. And following His resurrection, before He returns to His Father in heaven, he remains for forty days with His disciples. Should we not discover in this repeated occurrence of the number forty God's special method of education?

If in all of these events we are able to discover the common element connected with the number forty, we will most probably understand better also the meaning of the Lenten forty days by which the Church, in her motherly care, prepares her children for Easter.

Chapter 17: Lent

4. The forty days of the great flood ended in the covenant God contracted with Noah.

The two times forty days of Moses on the Mountain and the forty-year stay of God's people in the desert took place under the sign of the covenant of Sinai.

And what about Jesus' forty days of fasting in the desert? Whereas His baptism in the Jordan reminds us of the Hebrews' passage through the Red Sea, His forty days of fasting recalls the forty years of the wandering of God's people in the desert. Jesus' fast in the desert prepares the new and eternal Passover/Easter covenant, and His forty-day stay with His disciples after His resurrection introduces His elevation on the heavenly throne as the only Mediator between God and man.

The forty-days-long pilgrimage of Elijah takes the prophet back, both physically and spiritually, to the sources of the Mosaic covenant.

The forty days God allows the people of Nineveh through the prophet Jonah extends the blessings of the covenant to the pagan, Gentile Ninevites.

We can see that every period connected with the number forty is bound in one way or another with the covenant between God and man. A covenant between two persons can be called friendship. So, the periods of forty tell about the friendly relationship, the intimate closeness between God and His friends. All of the periods of forty are characterized by a temporary retreat from the created world. The Church, through her Lent, places the Christian people into this period of the biblical forty days so that the new and eternal covenant wrought by the death and resurrection of Jesus could be renewed.

5. How should we spend these holy forty days so that they would be for us truly fruitful?

We should step back somewhat from the world and get closer to God. If we withdraw ourselves a little bit from the world, God Himself will come to us in intimate closeness.

The Church recommends a triple exercise for Lent: fasting, prayer, and giving alms. Fasting signifies the desert, the withdrawal from the world. Prayer, *lectio divina* and meditation bring God close to us. But we cannot be close to God if we forget about our brothers and sisters. With our generous, helpful charity we serve Christ also in our neighbors. Fasting is possible not only by living on bread and water. Fasting has many forms, and we should choose the kind that fits best with our life situation and tests exactly the weak points of our personality. It may mean giving up something in food and drink, curtailing our time spent with entertainment, or performing some work or obligation that we usually start very reluctantly. Our program of *lectio divina* and prayer: Maybe during Lent we can lengthen somewhat the time dedicated to spiritual reading, spend more time before the Blessed Sacrament, and offer some extra devotion like the Stations of the Cross.

An old piece of Christian advice is to give to the poor whatever we save by our fasting. Fasting does not mean saving money for something to buy for ourselves, or dieting in order to lose weight. If we save time by our "fasting," dedicate this extra time to our brothers in need. Perhaps visit a sick father; talk to him a few minutes, holding his hands. Make some phone calls to needy friends or relatives. Let's be inventive, generous, and faithful in our Lenten exercises.

Remember the advice of St. Benedict in his *Rule*. He says that monks should live a holy life during the entire year, all 365 days of the year. However, since they are too weak to be faithful all the time throughout the whole year, the Church has given us this period of forty days, about the length of one tenth of a year. At least during the forty days of Lent let us try to live truly holy, exemplary Christian lives.

18

PRAYER

1. What makes a human being really human? There are many features that we share with animals: we need air to breathe, water to drink, and food to eat; we procreate, our bodies get sick and old, and in the end we die. Animals in some ways are even better than humans. The dog's sense of odor is a thousand times better than that of man; a cheetah runs faster than the fastest human, and so on. If so, what really makes us different from or superior to the animal world? Level of intelligence? The size of our brain? Is that what makes us "rational man," "thinking man," *homo sapiens*? Or the awareness of self, of our ego? Or the ability to think reflectively? Or the ability to improve ourselves and our achievements, our ability to learn?

    In 1952, the French author Jean Bruller (under the pseudonym Vercors) published a novel entitled *Les animaux dénaturés*. (The English versions of the book had the titles *You Shall Know Them*, *The Murder of the Missing Link*, and *Borderline*. A motion picture was also made of the book under the title *Skullduggery*.) It is a fiction story about a hypothetical situation: In a jungle of southeast Asia, a group of scientist-explorers find creatures who look like either animals with very high intelligence or humans with very low intelligence. Which are they? Are they humans or animals? After a long debate, the verdict is that they are animals. On what basis do the scientists make this decision? They notice that the creatures in the jungle are wearing no amulets, not any kind of good-luck-charm! There is no trace of any form of religion, no belief in or calling for help of a superior being. Therefore, the scientist-explorers deemed them to be animals. Signs of even the most primitive religion would have made them reverse their verdict—and to identify the creatures as human beings.

Indeed, it is an undeniable fact that neither anthropologists nor paleo-anthropologists have ever found tribes or communities of human beings who did not have some form of religion. Neanderthal people (about 100,000 years ago) buried their dead with weapons and food and covered them with flower petals: they had a belief in afterlife. The Cro-Magnon man (about 15,000 to 20,000 years ago) painted pictures of animals on walls of their dwelling caves to put a spell on them: they believed in the existence of supernatural power. Thus, we have to conclude that we humans are, first of all, *homo religiosus, homo orans,* religious man, praying man. Religion is the special feature, and praying is the special ability that lifts us above the animal world to the level of being truly human, made in the image and likeness of God.

2. In our human relationships, encounters can be two kinds: functional or personal. Functional is the encounter when the purpose of the encounter is outside the two persons who meet, when the only goal of the encounter is to obtain that "outside" purpose and the two persons only perform a function to obtain it. In this case the two persons who interact don't mean the least to each other; they just want to settle a transaction like buying or selling an item, or like offering or requesting a service. In a personal encounter, on the contrary, all that matters are the persons themselves who meet; in this case the identity of the persons is all-important because there is a bond that connects them, a bond of friendship or love. In this case the encounter itself is the goal; the presence of the other is what causes joy or happiness for both of them.

   This distinction is important in the context of prayer because many people get stuck in an immature, merely functional relationship with God. Such people pray only when they need something. For them, God is asked only to perform a function; God as person is unimportant. Our prayer life cannot consist of mere shopping lists. Of course, friends and lovers also ask favors from each other but such requests don't exhaust their relationship. Every way of living in a community like a family or religious community includes various chores, various forms of help, which at times may require great sacrifices. But these activities are not simply "functions." They are a variety of expressions of a personal love-relationship. The ultimate motivation in doing them is not simply to carry out a duty or obligation; rather, the ultimate motivation springs from love. In the same way, intercessory prayer should be an integral part of everyone's prayer life. But intercessory prayer is only one of several kinds of prayer. Prayer, in essence, is living a love-relationship with God, a living connection with God, a love-union with God.

In every personal encounter we exchange thoughts and ideas, and by listening to each other we grow in our mutual knowledge of each other. In learning about each other, not only the mind but also the heart is intimately involved. Also for prayer, growth in the knowledge of God (which can happen in several different ways) is vitally important. Especially in John's gospel, but also in other books of the Bible, love and knowledge are very closely related, at times, they are interchangeable, like in this statement of Jesus: "I know mine and mine know me" (Jn 10:4). Similarly, in Genesis, we find this concise remark: "Adam knew Eve his wife, and she conceived" (Gen 4:1 RSV). Knowledge in the biblical sense of the word means loving knowledge or knowing love; knowledge and love are very closely related; one supposes the other.

3. God decided to reveal Himself to human beings so that man could know and love Him. True knowledge of God can come about only on God's initiative. In the biblical stories of both the Old and the New Testament and also in the lives of the saints, God always takes the first step. It's not

man, curious and wondering about God, who rises up to God to learn about Him, to assimilate himself to Him. Rather, it is God, who, as if He were stepping out of Himself, approaches man to create contact, communion between the human person and Himself. "You did not choose me but I chose you," says Jesus (John 15:16); "We love [God], because he first loved us" (1 John 4:19).

If the infinite, all-powerful God can initiate an intimate relationship with a human being, if God can offer Himself to man for knowing and loving Him, then there must exist in us a center, a place, a *locus* where man can receive Him. This center, this "God-shaped hole" is the spot where we have been created, in particular, in the image and likeness of God. Living and loving on this level is where the person is most himself, living on this level man can find himself the most, can truly find his personal happiness and fulfillment, can fathom the meaning and goal of his very existence. That's where Augustine's "restless heart" finds its rest. We can say that beyond all other possible tasks, challenges, and goals of human life, man has been created first of all for the reception of God, for union with God. God is man's true environment and habitat. Although we're very limited beings, this ability to receive God into ourselves in a way lifts us beyond ourselves; we surpass ourselves. By this ability, we people living within the confines of space and time, touch God's eternity and infinity.

4. With another metaphor we can compare our inner depths to a beautiful chalice: the inner bottom of the cup is this center of our soul. Whatever happens higher above in our soul, closer to the rim, is all flowing down here. Everything gravitates toward this center. In fact, this center is the Temple of the Lord where God's presence is the strongest; it's here where His glory, His *"kabod,"* is shining. This is the place of love, the "King's chamber" of the Song of Songs (1:4). This is Mount Tabor where the Lord reveals His glory to His closest friends who say, "It is good for us to be here" (Mt 17:4). This is the Upper Room where, during the Last Supper, the beloved disciple rests his head on the Lord's breast, maybe even hears His heart beating. This is our real home; here we can truly "find rest" for our restless souls (cf. Mt 11:29; St. Augustine). This is the contemplative dimension of our existence, the contact point between earth and heaven, time and eternity. Let's love this place. Let's make it the place where we love to stay ("remain," "abide" in John) the most. Let's try to dwell here. Let's enjoy here our *"otium"* (rest) with God, just spend time here to *"vacare Deo"* (spend time with God). "A day in your courts is better than a thousand elsewhere; I would rather be a doorkeeper in the house of my God than dwell in the tents of the wicked" (Ps 84:10). Wherever our duties, needs, and charity may take us, let's always try to gravitate from those places toward this point as the deepest point of our person, as our home.

5. As we dwell ("abide," "remain") at this deepest point, let's spend our time before God, watch Him, listen to Him, taste Him, pay attention to Him, "experience" Him, with the simplicity of a child. Let us be like the old peasant who spent hours daily in the empty village church of St. John Vianney and, when St. John asked him what he was doing there so long, he answered, "I'm looking at Him, He's looking at me." This is true prayer. Let's continue at this point our never-ending I-Thou dialogue with God, our loving exchange with Him; let's listen to His words in our reflective *lectio divina* as Martha's sister Mary did, sitting at the feet of Jesus because this is indeed the "better part". Let's talk to Him from this depth of our hearts either with words or in the silence of the void or *"nada"* ("nothing" of St. Teresa of Avila) as the vessel that is filled with God to the brim. Let's allow also all our pains and joys, sorrows and occasional relief, troubles and cheers descend here. Let's bring here everything that bothers us or inspires us or attracts us or repels us. Let this be the place where we are fed, recharged, and energized; let it be our source of energy, persistence, endurance, and vitality. Let here the living waters of the Holy Spirit well up inside us like a fountain to quench not only <u>our</u> thirst but also that of other people. Then the miracle at the wedding in Cana will happen again: the water will turn into wine and the Paschal mystery will take place. Then we realize that this chalice is actually the cup or Grail and the wine, with all our joys and crosses, is the Blood of Jesus. Then we understand that our

prayer life is actually the continuous Eucharist of our lives when (like the disciples of Emmaus) we'll recognize the Lord in the breaking of the bread.

6. To define what prayer really is, a key word is "contact" or "connection." Just as light bulbs will light up and machines and appliances will turn on only if they are in contact with the electric powerhouse, the praying person must get and remain in contact with the Lord, in a contact that is fueled by faith, hope, and love—mainly by love. This contact must be a lived reality, a reality that can be illustrated by phrases like to be "in eye contact with Jesus" or to be in a "person to person" connection with Him. The praying person must be "paying attention" and "listening" to Him ("*Ausculta, O fili*...Listen, O son," the first words in the Prologue of the *Rule* of St. Benedict). We can say that by sanctifying grace we are in a constant habitual contact with God, and by prayer this habitual contact becomes an actual contact. Prayer is the actualization of sanctifying grace, God's Trinitarian life present in us. By prayer we allow this grace to work in us to its full "capacity". We allow the current of Trinitarian life flow abundantly into us and through us.

We can use also another key word for prayer: "presence." Prayer is a "total presence" with the Lord, a prolonged, conscious "abiding" in the Lord's presence. For this "total presence" we could use also the term employed for meditation by Jessica C. Kraft in her article *Quiet Your*

Mind—"complete absorption." We concentrate on God so that we are completely present to Him. I suppose that this aspect of focusing on the presence of God is also what the Trappist celebrities Thomas Merton and Basil Pennington meant by "centering prayer," the form of prayer that became so popular in America. This kind of prayer can be done anywhere, any time, and in any situation. For a Christian, there should be no empty or wasted time. We can put ourselves in the presence of God wherever we are—while waiting in a doctor's office or in a grocery-store line, while exercising, or while driving alone on the highway.

7. If we understand prayer in this context we realize also what Christian existence is or should be: we are living "in" Christ, we dwell in Him, He surrounds us as our atmosphere, as our clothing. St. Paul likes to use this formula: "If anyone is in Christ, he is a new creation" (2 Cor 5:17), or "There is no condemnation for those who are in Christ Jesus" (Rom 8:1). What St. Paul stated at Areopagus in Athens about our relationship to God applies perfectly also to our relationship with Christ: "In Him we live and move and have our being" (Act 17:28). Christ is our "divine milieu," our true habitat, our life-supporting environment. Understanding Christian life in this way, we can see that a Christian's whole day, whole life is prayer or at least a prayerful, prayer-like existence: "So, whether you eat or drink, or whatever you do, do all for the glory of God"

(1Cor 10:31). When we live with this kind of attitude, our lives become non-stop prayer: "Rejoice always, pray constantly, give thanks in all circumstances" (1Thess 5:16-18).

In our activities the all-important and essential ingredient is love; if we do everything with love, everything becomes prayer. The love of Christ penetrates all our activities, and transforms them into prayer. "If a needy person requires medicine or other help during prayer time, do whatever has to be done with peace of mind. Offer the deed to God as your prayer. Do not become upset or feel guilty because you interrupted your prayer to serve the poor. God is not neglected if you leave him for such service. One of God's works is merely interrupted so that another can be carried out" (St. Vincent de Paul).

8. There is a fundamental dynamic tension in every authentic Christian existence. We experience alternately at times God's call to draw us near Him and at other times His sending us away to other people. Consider these two groups of quotes from the gospels:

   a) The call into Christ's solitude: "When you pray, go into your room and shut the door and pray to your Father who is in secret" (Mt 6:6). "Come to me, all who labor and are heavy laden, and I will give you rest" (Mt 11:28). When the apostles return from a pastoral mission, Jesus says to them, "Come away by yourselves to a deserted place, and rest a while"

(Mk 6:31). In John he says, "If a man loves me, he will keep my word, and my Father will love him, and we will come to him and make our home with him" (14:23). Later in John He says, "I made known to them your name, and I will make it known, that the love with which you loved me, may be in them, and I in them" (17:26).

b) The sending to others: "Go therefore and make disciples of all nations" (Mt 28:19). "As you [Father] sent me into the world, so I sent them into the world" (John 17:18); "As the Father has sent me, even so I send you" (John 20:21).

A double vocation is echoing in the heart of every Christian, a vocation that is an integral component in every Christian life. Christ is calling us to Himself into an intimate personal relationship, and Christ is sending us into the world to proclaim His good news to other people. Every Christian receives this double vocation of prayerful contemplation and apostolic mission. This tension never leaves us, never lets us rest in a happy idleness. It's a sign of spiritual well-being if the Christian experiences a constant homesickness: when we pray, we long to go among our brothers and sisters to talk to them about God whose closeness we've just experienced, and while we are in the midst of people during good work, we hunger and thirst for solitude, to stay alone in union with God. Neither of these two poles can be excluded. Without a deep personal prayer life there cannot be any true apostolic work, and without apostolic zeal there is no true contemplation. In the life of the soul there are two forces operating in harmony with each other: a centripetal force (moving toward the center) and a centrifugal force (moving away from a center). It's like the pendulum of a grandfather clock: for the normal operation of the clock it is indispensable that the pendulum keeps swinging regularly back and forth, that this constant oscillation keeps on going. This special feature of Christian life follows logically from the two-fold Great Commandment concerning the love of God and the love of neighbor. One love cannot exist without the other. "If anyone says, 'I love God,' and hates his brother, he is a liar" (1 John 4:20). The proportion of the two elements in any individual Christian life may vary but neither of the two poles can be neglected or excluded. In a Carthusian monk's life, the emphasis is evidently on the side of contemplation. In a Jesuit's way of life, the stress is on the apostolic work. Only this difference in the proportion of prayer and apostolic work distinguishes from each other the so called "contemplative" and "active" religious orders. Yet, while both poles are indispensable parts of Christian life, the primacy evidently belongs to the love of God, to the element of prayer. One can speak about God to others only if his heart and soul have been already filled with the presence of God. People can recognize Christ in the person of the apostle only if his whole being has been penetrated and imbued by Christ through frequent personal prayer.

This means that ultimately neither "pure" *vita contemplativa* nor "pure" *vita activa* exists: every authentic Christian life is a *vita mixta*, a combination of both prayer and apostolate.

9. Prayer is the breathing of the soul. What air is for the body, prayer is for the soul. Without oxygen the body cannot live; in the same way, without prayer the soul cannot live. The popular philosopher author Peter Kreeft uses a similar image: "Eating keeps your body alive, and prayer keeps your soul alive. Praying is more important than eating because your soul is more important than your body" (*Prayer for Beginners*, p. 11). A devout prayer life is not only important but also indispensable for the life of the soul. A Christian without prayer is a total anomaly, an absolute contradiction. Prayer for the life of the soul is a condition *sine qua non*. St Paul says, "Pray without ceasing!" (1 Thess 5:17). Of course, we cannot be on our knees 24/7, but we can keep in our mind a constant prayerful attitude. Prayer is like the cell phone: you can use it at any place, at any time. Forty years ago nobody had a cell phone; today nobody can imagine his or her life without it. We cannot imagine our spiritual life without prayer. Prayers should go up to God nonstop like the beat of our hearts. Whatever happens during our days, we can remain connected with God by short prayers like "Thank you, Lord!" "I love you, Lord!" "Please help me now!" "Please forgive me!" or just by repeating the

sacred name of Jesus. Prayer is nothing else than a constant, intimate connection with God.

19

DO NOT JUDGE

1. The human mind, by its very nature, is always searching for the truth and when it finds something that is true or correct, it expresses this truth in a statement, what the science of logics calls a judgment. We received from God our intellectual abilities so that with their help we can establish and put into a verbal statement the truth we have found in the form of a judgment. To abstain from any kind of judgment would be contrary to the nature of human intellect.

   Yet, Jesus, in the Sermon on the Mount, expressed in no ambiguous terms that we should not judge. He said, "Stop judging that you may not be judged. For as you judge, so you will be judged, and the measure with which you measure will be measured out to you. Why do you notice the splinter in your brother's eye, but do not perceive the wooden beam in your own eye?" (Mt 7:1-3)

   Do Jesus' words mean that we should refrain from ever making an assertion about something that we think is true? Certainly not. But the character of various truths can be different. It is one thing to find and explain mathematical, astronomical, or any other objective scientific truths; however, it is another thing to form a judgment about a person's actions, intentions, or personality. Original sin obscured the eyes of our mind and contaminated our ability to make valid judgments about other people. We are still able to keep our sight clear and unbiased for objective facts about the world around us, but our minds can be easily clouded when we try to judge and make a statement about a person's isolated acts or about that person's inner attitude or moral character. We are very easily inclined to accuse someone wrongly without sufficient evidence, to evaluate someone's deeds or words in a negative way. Thus, when Jesus says, "Do not judge," he means that we should not judge people.

This is also the way the apostle James understood our Lord's words as he was reflecting on judging in his letter: "Whoever speaks evil of a brother or judges his brother, speaks evil of the law and judges the law. If you judge the law, you are not a doer of the law but a judge. There is one lawgiver and judge who is able to save or to destroy. Why then are you to judge your neighbor?" (James 4:11-12). Concerning our feelings about people, we should rather be suspicious of our own suspicions, be critical of our criticism, and accuse ourselves for falsely accusing others. We should have a basic skeptical attitude about our gut-feelings about other people, and have a cautiously critical stance toward everything our instincts suggest concerning words and deeds and behavior of other human beings. Only God can make an absolutely correct judgment about a person's thoughts, deeds, and character.

Chapter 19: Do Not Judge

Let's take a closer look at our urges to judge, criticize and condemn others: Why are we doing it? What's wrong with it? What are the alternatives? What follows here does not try to be a "treatise" on the topic: it will be just a series of vignettes of various observations about judging other people.

2. Some Christians who, though they are aware of Jesus' words to avoid judging our fellowmen, try to justify their critical attitude by saying, "To take note of and to make known the truth about other people is more important than anything else." They may even quote the Bible: "And you will know the truth, and the truth will set you free" (John 8:32). An obvious objection to such a statement would be probably another quote from the gospel of St. John: "Pilate said to him: 'What is truth?' " (John 18:38).

It has been said that when looking at an iceberg, one can see just about one tenth of the entire bulk of ice; the rest is submerged. When we see someone acting in a certain way, before we formulate an opinion about it, we should realize that in this case we see actually an even smaller fraction of the whole reality than in the case of an iceberg. Even if the visible action is evidently wrong, what can we know about the person's true intentions, about his or her freedom in doing it, about the complex web of partly conscious, partly subconscious motivations of the act? Yet, the real moral weight of an action is determined not so much by the visible act than by the true intention, the amount of freedom, and the secret motivations of the person who did the act. We are simply not in the position to judge fairly anyone's actions or character. It is only God who can see the entire mind and heart of the person, and thus only God can give a valid judgment about the moral character of an action. This means that whenever we judge other people, we try to "play God" by putting ourselves in God's seat of judgment and doing what He alone can validly do.

3. Another response to a person demanding the right to criticize someone in the name of the truth should be that mercy is more important than truth or justice. As the Latin adage says, "*Summum jus summa injuria*; The full exercise of one's rights can be the fullness of injustice." Aggressive lawyers, for example, try to find a loophole which <u>seems</u> to be a promotion of justice but in fact is a miscarriage of justice. We should rather follow the principle: Hate the sin, love the sinner. This is a well-known statement but it's hard to practice. We have to separate in our mind the person who acts and the act itself. An action that is evidently sinful we have to reject but we may not cast away the person; it is as if we are saying, "I hate what you are doing but I love you nevertheless." We have to make this distinction with every wrongdoer, even with our enemy, even if he did the wrong against us. This is the attitude inspired by the Beatitudes. "Be merciful, just as your Father is merciful" (Luke 6:36). This is the gospel spirit of Jesus, who from His

cross was praying for His executioners. We must extend and apply this principle also on our judgmental attitude. We may condemn an evidently wrong or sinful deed, but we still have to extend our love toward the person who committed it. Pope Francis could have the nickname "the pope of mercy" because mercy is the theme of so many of his pronouncements. Or think of Pope St. John Paul II who visited in the prison the man who tried to assassinate him, and forgave him.

4. As we know, an automobile is a wonderful invention but it can also be a murder weapon. In the same way, words as a means of communication can express love and transmit information but they can also wound or even kill. Author William Chapman wrote, "Words cut deeper than knives. A knife can be pulled out; words are embedded into our souls." We read in the letter of St. James: "Consider how small a fire can set a huge forest ablaze. The tongue is also a fire" (3:5-6). The tongue is like a knife or like fire. The knife is a useful tool, but it can be a dangerous lethal weapon. The fire is absolutely necessary for life, but it can be the most destructive of all calamities. St. James continues his letter: "No human being can tame the tongue. It is a restless evil, full of deadly poison. With it we bless the Lord and Father, and with it we curse human beings who are made in the likeness of God" (3:8-9). Words can be a blessing and a curse. We should spread around us only good words, never bad ones. We are responsible for other

people's reputations. When talking about a person to somebody else, by our words we should improve that person's renown, not diminish it. Backbiting or critical, disparaging remarks damage the opinion about that person whereas, as a rule of thumb, our job as a Christian is to create a more favorable view.

5. We know from experience that for our own mistakes, sins, and failures we can always find excuses, explanations, pretexts, or at least some alleviating circumstances. If we can be so lenient and understanding toward ourselves, why do we try to be so cruelly strict and outright merciless, in the name of objectivity in enunciating a verdict over other people?

László Mécs, a Norbertine priest and poet in twentieth-century Hungary, wrote among hundreds of other lyrics a collection of beautiful poems about motherhood. In one of these poems entitled "The Three Sorrows of the Prince," he speaks about his own mother. Here is a short section of it in translation:

> When I was born,
> no strange stars signaled a Messiah:
> only my mother knew that I was a prince.
>
> Others saw only a crying brat
> but my mother covered me with swaddling rags
> as if she were fondling the beautiful sun itself.

> As long as she is alive, I can live happily,
> I have everything in the world, and I miss nothing --
> yet I'm troubled by three sorrows.
>
> My first sorrow:
> why can't other people, the many princes and princesses,
> see each other as their mother saw them?
>
> My second sorrow:
> when she'll rest lifeless in the tomb and will become a flower,
> no one will know that I'm a prince.

Yes, why can't we see others as their mothers see them? Why can't we be a little biased in favor of the person in whom we find some imperfection? When we see that these "princes" and "princesses" are doing something wrong, why can't we find excuses for their actions as their mother would? We should have an attitude of basic benevolence and goodwill, a basic friendly disposition toward each person we meet.

6. We have to admit that we do criticize people as frequently as we do because it just "feels <u>so</u> good." As Bishop Robert Barron says, "We delight in pointing out the shortcomings, moral failings, and annoying tendencies of our neighbors. This is, of course, a function of pride and egotism: the

more I put someone else down, the more elevated I feel." When we talk about other people's blunders, we have the (false) impression that we are better than they are and that we would "never sink as low as they did." We forget so easily that in reality we're not better at all, that maybe we are just as "bad" or even worse than the person we criticized. Whenever we feel the urge to judge someone in a negative way and so to experience our imaginary superiority, we should remind ourselves that we are not perfect either, that we are also sinners, maybe worse than the person we criticize. We should take seriously the question of Jesus: "Why do you notice the splinter in your brother's eye, but do not perceive the wooden beam in your own eye?" (Mt 7:3). Maybe the answer to this question is that exactly this wooden beam blinds us to see ourselves as we really are.

7. Let's go back to the Sermon on the Mount. It's interesting to observe that Jesus' statement in Matthew, "Be perfect as your heavenly Father is perfect" (Mt 5:48), is formulated differently in Luke's Sermon on the Plain: "Be merciful just as your Father is merciful" (Lk 6:36). First of all, the double exhortation is a really tall order: the measure of our being "perfect" and "merciful" is set as high as the perfection and mercy of the Father Himself. Obviously, this goal can be achieved even in the smallest degree only by God's constant help, an extra-large dose of grace, and may take an entire lifetime. But, looking at it from a different angle, it seems to be logical: Children usually look like their father

or mother. If, as Jesus revealed it, God is truly not only our Maker but our Father who gives us a share in His own divine nature, if we really try to act to be seen really as His children, it logically follows that in our personalities, attitudes, and actions we should reflect the "character features" of God Himself.

Second, from the texts of Matthew and Luke it seems that being "perfect" and being "merciful" are two characteristics of God that are interchangeable; the most important attribute of God's perfection is exactly His merciful Love, His Divine Mercy. "God is Love" (1 John 4:8), St. John says in his letter. We all remember Jesus' parable of the wicked servant who immediately after his master forgave his debt of an immense sum, cruelly demanded payment from a fellow servant who owed him just a small fraction of the debt he had owed his master. If we wish to find mercy with God, we just have to follow the Beatitudes. We have to practice mercy: "Blessed are the merciful, for they will be shown mercy" (Matthew 5:7). If we practice the Golden Rule, "Do to others whatever you would have them do to you" (Matthew 7:12), then a sinner like me, who has been forgiven by God a tremendous amount of debt of sin, must forgive the hurt or even great damage that another person may have caused me. Thus, what the Sermon on the Mount demands of us concerning criticizing people is a simple application of the Golden Rule: "Stop judging that you may not be judged. For as you judge, so you will be judged, and the measure with which you measure will be measured out to you" (Matthew 7:1-2). The same principle is expressed in the letter of James: "Do not complain, brothers, about one another, that you may not be judged. Behold, the Judge is standing before the gates" (5:9). Yes, the final judgment, the *Parousia,* is imminent!

8. There are also some very subtle ways of criticizing others, but exactly because of their subtleness these kinds of criticism are even more devious than other manifestations of it. Let me mentions two of them.

    First, in a conversation one may avoid directly criticizing someone but can cleverly direct the exchange of thoughts toward a certain person. He can induce his conversation partner to say critical remarks about that person while he, the one who started the conversation, just stands by "innocently" and looks disapprovingly scandalized. He enjoys hearing the malicious gossip without adding one demeaning word.

    Another kind of criticism may happen even in the presence of the one who is being criticized. Someone in the group may talk about an unnamed third person and say disparaging remarks about him. All those present soon realize the obvious similarity between the person who is anonymously criticized and the one who may or may not be present.

9. There are some professional people whose job is to find mistakes, errors, and faults, like quality controllers. There

Chapter 19: Do Not Judge

are superiors who must notice and deal with his or her subject's shortcomings, and officials whose duty is to find out whether someone did a criminal act or not (detectives, district attorneys, judges). Such people are only a small fraction of society. Yet almost everyone likes to <u>act</u> as a judge. Why do people act like "quality controllers" and look constantly for mistakes if it is not their job and none of their business? Why do they prefer to look for what is wrong in people rather than what is right?

Take a Persian rug, a beautiful creation of human hands. As beautiful as it is, no human product is absolutely perfect. There are a number of imperfections, small faulty spots, even on a precious Persian rug. Its gifted makers made them almost invisible, by hiding them on the bottom side. The top side dazzles us in its perfect beauty. The wise person looks at the top side of the rug and enjoys it, while the foolish one looks at the bottom side and points out the few imperfections with bitter criticism, bragging about how smart he is. People also have their "right" side and "wrong" side, their positive and their negative features. Every person has a shadow. Why would one deprive himself of enjoying the beauty of the right side and choose to look only for the faults on the wrong side?

10. It happens quite frequently that what we judge to be wrong is not, in reality, wrong at all but different. Most results in our world can be obtained in a great variety of ways. One can arrive at a destination by taking one of a number of

different routes. We have the tendency to believe that <u>my</u> way is the only right way, and all the other ways are wrong – which obviously cannot be true. We should not become so narrow-minded that we judge anything wrong that is not according to our personal taste. We should rather constantly widen and enlarge our hearts to make room there for many people so that we allow them to be themselves no matter how different they or their tastes may be. It's exactly the great variety of people that makes the world beautiful. Imagine if everybody around you were a carbon copy of yourself, having the same personality, same character, same habits, and same taste: what a terribly boring world that would be!

Yes, we are different and sometimes different personalities clash. People can have conflicting personalities. Such conflicts usually arise for two reasons: the other person is either too much like me or too different. It can happen that in a person we see our own shortcomings "incarnated" and we don't like it, and therefore we don't like the person who carries them either. The opposite happens when an introvert cannot stand a non-stop talker, or a more outgoing person may look at the timid guy as a wimp, or a jock may think of a bookworm as a nerd. Then there are also some eccentric or particular persons who may irritate most people. It's here again that the principle of forgiveness enters. We must be able to "forgive" people for being different, for irritating us by their very existence;

we must forgive for the simple reason that they are not responsible for the personality they have. We must try hard to accept and embrace every human being even if he or she happens to be a disagreeable or nasty personality; we should pray to become generous enough to welcome in our hearts every type of person.

11. Many times somebody criticizes a person's natural endowments, natural abilities, and characteristics for which the person is not responsible at all and which, probably, are an affliction and a heavy cross for the person to carry. These can be physical features or handicaps, mental limitations, and cases when someone is "challenged" in some way. To prey on other people's weaknesses would be the lowest kind of criticizing others or making fun of them.

    Stop constantly looking at others and comparing yourself with them, trying to find them at fault or amiss in something. Don't give in to your urge of curiosity. Let them be. Let them be themselves. Let them be loved.

12. How can we avoid being critical or judgmental toward others? Judgments, critical remarks are only the symptoms; we have to go to the roots of evil remarks. Criticism, uncharitable judgments originate in our hearts. Jesus said, "The things that come out of the mouth come from the heart, and they defile. For from the heart come evil thoughts. [...] These are what defile a person, but to eat with unwashed hands does not defile" (Matthew 15:18-20).

We must stop judging others at the first instance when such thought arises in our mind. Our attitude depends on how we look at others at the first moment we see them or think of them, whether our eyes are welcoming or rejecting the person. We should have a hospitable personality; we should be a person in whose presence everyone can feel welcome and safe. We know some people who have a hospitable personality; we should imitate them, follow their example. We judge others in the way we think of them in the depth of our hearts. We should discover the positive features in others and appreciate them; we should find out what makes them likable, attractive. We have to look for these features in them and make a mental note of them. Look for the goodness in them. Think good thoughts. We should think kind thoughts about everyone. From such thoughts good judgments will rise. We should look at everybody with benevolence. Anticipate goodwill from everyone. It is a good rule of thumb that most people usually show themselves to be whatever we expect from them. Hostility will provoke hostility while friendliness calls forward friendliness. Every human being has been made in the image and likeness of God. Discover God's fingerprint on everyone.

It's also good advice not to avoid the company of a person who irritates us or whom we like to criticize: we should rather seek his company, spend time in his presence, because if we stay away from such a person, his negative traits tend to grow in our minds. We will see him more and more in a negative light, and sooner or later he may become a monster in our consciousness. Meeting him rather frequently will keep him in a human size. We will perceive him as a struggling human being, and we will more easily notice also his good characteristics.

Finally, we should foster in our soul and mind a good sense of humor. We should not take other people's idiosyncrasies so seriously. Instead of becoming angry and upset about their shortcomings, we should rather smile at their strange words and actions with generous understanding, forbearance, and tolerance. We should look at other people's weaknesses with love. "Love is patient, love is kind" (1 Cor 13:4). We should take to heart the words of St. Mother Teresa of Calcutta: "If you judge people, you have no time to love them."

20

HOLY THURSDAY

The gospel reading on Holy Thursday tells the story of Jesus washing the feet of his apostles at the Last Supper. We might expect that it would be more fitting to read on Holy Thursday the account of the institution of the Holy Eucharist, since, after all, this is what we celebrate on the first day of the Easter Triduum. The reason for this reading selection may be that it opens the whole section of John's gospel describing Jesus' trial, suffering, and death, which is a major, almost independent unit of John's gospel. The washing of the feet is Jesus' prophetic action explaining the meaning of His approaching sufferings and death: Jesus is showing that He is the humble servant-leader who performs the slave's job not only for the apostles but also for the entire human race. By this act He opens the way of salvation for all those who believe in Him.

Although the whole passage has this introductory character and purpose, the first verse is a particularly important preliminary statement. The first verse of chapter 13 solemnly announces, "Before the feast of Passover, Jesus knew that his hour has come to pass from this world to the Father. He loved his own in the world and he loved them to the end." Let us meditate on this verse containing three key words: (1) Passover, (2) His hour, (3) love.

(1) "Before the feast of <u>Passover</u>." Jesus' suffering and death took place on the eve of the greatest Jewish feast, Passover. The name "Passover" designates two redeeming divine acts: First, on Passover night when all the firstborn male children of the Egyptians died, the destroying angel "passed over" the houses of the Hebrews which were marked with the blood of the Passover lamb. In those houses nobody died. Second, the name marks the event when the Hebrews miraculously "passed over," that is, crossed the Red Sea from slavery into freedom and when the Egyptians pursuing them were destroyed. Now, at the new Passover, Jesus, and we, His disciples with Him, will pass from this world, which is enslaved by sin, to the Father's company, the true Promised Land. Passover means liberation from the slavery of sin. The Jewish Law, the Torah prescribed that each year at Passover every Jewish family had to sacrifice a lamb in the Temple and consume it at a solemn Passover meal in memory of their liberation from slavery in Egypt. Jesus' arrest, trial, and execution coincided with this Jewish feast and celebration. This was the day and the hour when Jesus, the Savior of the human race, had to "pass from this world to the Father." The Passover feast that year fell on a Sabbath, and on the eve of this Sabbath-Passover Jesus was executed on Calvary Hill at the same time that the heads

of Jewish families took the sacrificial lamb to the Temple for the sacrifice. Jesus' death coincided with the sacrifice of the Passover lambs, signifying that Jesus Himself is the true Lamb of God whose blood saves us from dying. Jesus died on the eve of Passover and spent the Sabbath-rest in the tomb, to rise from the dead as new creation, as new Adam, on Sunday, the first day of creation.

(2) "Jesus knew that His hour has come to pass from this world to the Father." Jesus' own Passover had to take place at a specific time, and this specific time was called His "hour." This "hour" is the most important in Jesus' whole life. The Son of God became man in the person of Jesus Christ for the purpose of this "hour." In the gospels, Jesus spoke several times about his "hour." At the wedding in Cana, when His mother Mary hinted that their hosts ran out of wine, Jesus answered that His "hour" has not yet come. The ancient Greeks had two words for time, *chronos* and *kairos*. Similarly, in the Greek New Testament, the authors use these two different terms for the concept of "time" with two specific meanings. For the common, everyday time they apply the word *chronos,* meaning the passing, chronological time. The other term, *kairos*, is an ancient Greek word meaning the right or opportune moment, the "supreme" moment. While *chronos* is quantitative, *kairos*

has a qualitative, permanent nature. In the New Testament *kairos* means "the appointed time in the purpose of God," the time when God acts (e.g., Mark 1.15, the *kairos* is fulfilled). *Kairos* (used approximately 81 times in the New Testament) seems to be an indeterminate time, a "moment" or a "season" of salvation whereas *chronos* (used 54 times) refers to a specific amount of time. In the New Testament, *kairos* has the specific meaning of the "time of salvation" when God intervenes in the earthly events, when God's eternity, heaven itself breaks through the category of the common passage of time and salvation takes place. Jesus' "hour" is the "now," the supreme *kairos*, the fulfillment of all the prophetic promises made through the centuries, the consummation of the final and eternal covenant between God and His people. This "hour" is one event in Jesus' life in two steps: first, the Last Supper at which Jesus offered Himself to the Father and gave His disciples His own Body and Blood in the form of bread and wine, as a perpetual memorial of this most important moment of history; and second, Jesus' actual agony and dying on the Cross.

(3) "He loved his own in the world and he loved them to the end." Jesus loved. Why does Jesus wash the feet of His apostles? Why does He hide Himself in the species

of bread and wine? Why does He take all the humiliation, torture, pain, and death on Himself? The only answer to these questions is that Jesus "loved His own in the world." Love is the final answer to everything; love is the beginning, and love is the end, the terminus, the arrival, the home. Love is all. Love is the ultimate motivation of everything Jesus is doing and allows to be done to Him in His supreme "hour." "He loved them to the end." Jesus is all love, unlimited love, unlimited in every sense of the world, unlimited in time, in measure. His love is all-encompassing. Nobody is left out, for it extends to every human being of every country at all times. All that John wrote about love in his gospel and in his letters applies here. "God is love, and whoever remains in love, remains in God and God in Him" (1 John 4:16). All that was flowing from Paul's pen in praise of love has its fulfillment here. "Love never fails. […] So faith, hope, love remain, these three; but the greatest of these is love" (1 Cor 8.13).

The New American Bible divides the gospel of John into four parts. The first 18 verses of Chapter 1 are the Prologue, followed by the rest of Chapter 1 up to Chapter 12: this section is called The Book of Signs. Chapters 13 through 20 have the title The Book of Glory. The concluding Chapter 21 is the Epilogue. The third part tells the story of Jesus' utter humiliation and suffering by the cruelest torture and agonizing death by crucifixion. Someone may ask, how can it be called <u>The Book of Glory</u>? The answer to this question was given by Jesus Himself when he said just before entering into his hour: "The hour has come for the Son of Man to be glorified" (John 12:23). Yes, the Passion of Jesus ends with the glory of His resurrection. Jesus' suffering and resurrection should not be considered separately: They are the two integral parts of the same one glorious mystery of the salvation of the human race. The glory shines through even through the darkest hour, <u>the</u> Hour of the earthly life of Jesus Christ the Redeemer. And the best news is that His glory is also our glory. Everything happened for our sake.

21

SUFFERING

In his classic novel *The Brothers Karamazov*, the great Russian novelist Fyodor Dostoyevsky is constantly struggling with the agonizing question why do innocent people have to suffer. His example for the innocent sufferer is a five-year-old child at whom an evil boyar (land owner) lets loose his ferocious hunting dogs and they maul the child to death. The little one had never hurt anyone in his short life: why did he have to suffer such a terrible death? We hear and read every day horrendous stories of crime, wars, terrorism, illness, accidents, - tragedies in which innocent people suffer. Why do we have to suffer? Is there an answer to this "Why"?

The old Cistercian abbot in Hungary, Wendelin Endrédy was arrested in 1950 by the communist government, was tortured cruelly, and spent seven years in prison, in solitary confinement. In 1957 he was released from prison and put in a house arrest in the country's only monastery. At the end of his long life he said that the most precious years of his life were the ones that he spent in prison. How can a person say such a thing?

I collected ten examples from everyday life which, maybe, can, at least partially, explain why we have to carry our crosses, why human sufferings are not completely senseless but, at times, may be even necessary.

1. A good father, a good educator is strict and demanding, sets high standards for his children or students. If it's needed, he even punishes those under his care. We read in the Bible that a good father disciplines his son even with the rod if needed. "He who spares his rod hates his son, but he who loves him takes care to chastise him" (Prov 13:24). The letter to the Hebrews states that even Christ learned obedience from what he had to suffer (5:8). Moral: Suffering is a means of <u>education</u>.

2. Growing children frequently experience growing pains. Growing up is a painful process. But, while the growth of the body may take just about twenty years, our spiritual growth continues until we die, and the growing pain does accompany it. Most of our inner growth consists in the growing realization that the image we have about ourselves is false, a distorted image, an illusion, and we have to face and accept gradually the reality who we are: our weaknesses, our limitations, our sinfulness and guilt, and this truth hurts. Moral: Much of the pain we experience is <u>growing pain</u>.

3. The next example is taken from the field of sports and military life. A good coach, a good sergeant must be tough to the point of cruelty because toughness in <u>training</u>, even inflicting a lot of pain, will bring out the best results of the

trainees and to make them winning athletes, invincible soldiers. St. Paul uses the image of athletes (like runners and boxers) and of soldiers in his letters to drive home the point that sacrifices are necessary for excellent achievements. Setting high goals, like climbing Mt. Everest or running a marathon involves a lot of previous training and very high costs in endurance and exertion. Moral: God is the best coach and trainer: He is so tough because he loves us.

4. If one is ill, the healing process involves considerable discomfort or pain: beginning (1) with a "bitter pill" or (2) extracting a tooth up to a (3) major surgery (loss of blood), including the process of (4) recovery and (5) rehab after a surgery, are all trying and painful experiences; yet, their purpose is not to inflict pain but to heal. Sometimes the smaller affliction is prophylactic: the smallpox vaccine gives you a mild degree of the illness itself to make you immune to prevent contracting the major disease. Moral: Sometimes suffering is actually God's <u>healing</u> power at work.

5. Precious metals like gold or silver are not found in nature in pure form; the ore containing that metal has to be heated up to a very high temperature and smelted to separate impurities from pure metal. Moral: When you suffer physical, mental, or emotional pain, maybe God just wants to <u>purify</u>

you from your selfishness to make you more like Himself, more worthy of Him.

6. Fruit trees need to be pruned so that they could produce more fruit. Pruning means to cut off superfluous (although healthy) branches that don't produce fruit so that they would not take away nourishment from the fruit-bearing branches and that all the sap, life-giving energy would go into the productive branches, in order to have the tree produce more fruit. Cruel activity? But it's for the benefit of the tree. Grafting to improve the fruit. Moral: Suffering is God's <u>pruning</u> process.

7. To produce the best quality of steel, the metal needs to be tempered at a very high temperature and by heavy hammering. Also to give to iron a specific shape like horseshoe, plow, or sword, the metal has to be made red hot and shaped with many blows of hammer, so that is would obtain the desired usefulness or beauty. Moral: Suffering is a process of <u>tempering</u> to make us the best quality, the most valuable product.

8. Giving birth can be very painful, yet to give life to a new baby is unmeasurable joy. Moral: every kind of suffering can be considered the pain of <u>giving birth</u> to something beautiful and valuable.

9. Pain produces beauty: A beautiful <u>pearl</u> is the product of pain, the pain of the soft body of the shell: the pearl is actually a "petrified" tear of the shell: when a speck of sand enters the inside of a shall, the pain caused by that speck produces some tissue fluid that hardens around that speck: the pearl is born and its growth will continue. Moral: External events can enter our lives and cause pain, but the result will be something precious.

10. When the construction of a new bridge is completed, before it would be opened for the public, a weight test will be performed. The structure will be loaded with objects of the multiple of the weight that the bridge would normally carry, and carefully checked whether the bridge shows any damage under such excessive weight. This is how it's established that the bridge is safe. A new brand of car is tested by driving it at maximum speed and giving it the worst abuse to see its endurance. Moral: Sometimes God may <u>test our endurance</u> and see how much we love Him.

Up to this point, I was trying to use images as illustrations to show that the crosses we have to carry are not completely meaningless. But we have to go beyond metaphors and analogies: we have to get through to the center: Why do we have to suffer? The ultimate reason of accepting pain, trial, hardships, even agonies in our life here on earth comes from the nature of love. There is no love without pain. The canonized Italian mother of a family, St.

Gianna Beretta Molla, boldly states: "One cannot love without suffering or suffer without loving." To take painful sacrifice is the test and the proof of authentic love. St. Peter, in his first letter, encourages Christians not just to accept suffering generously but to rejoice in suffering: "Rejoice in so far as you share Christ's sufferings, that you may also rejoice and be glad when his glory is revealed" (1 Peter 4:13). St. Paul is a witness that such a joy is possible; he writes to the Colossians: "I rejoice in my sufferings for your sake, and in my flesh I complete what is lacking in Christ's afflictions for the sake of his body, that is, the church" (Col 1:24). Love leads a person to give up his most precious treasures: to give up wealth, loved ones, health, even life itself. A soldier gives his life out of love of his country. Parents are ready to give anything for the recovery of a sick child. By accepting suffering and pain we show God that what we love is God Himself, not just His gifts or consolations. Jesus not only set this rule for His followers but also demonstrated it in His own person: "No one has greater love than this, to lay down one's life for one's friends" (John 15:13). Someone who loves would take over happily the pain of his loved one. Christ gave the best example for such vicarious suffering and death by His passion and death on the cross, and many Christians followed His example; just think of St. Maximilian Kolbe who, in the concentration camp of Auschwitz volunteered to die in place of his fellow prisoner, a Jewish family man. But we should never forget: "Love is strong as death" (Song 8:6, NEB); Jesus proved that by His own resurrection. Moral: many times pain and suffering is a test of our love and such suffering with or instead of others has redeeming value if we unite our crosses with the Cross of Christ.

God's love, God's treasury of graces knows no limits; yet, the capacity of our hearts to receive this love is very small. God wishes to give as much a share of His love as possible, because He knows that the greater love we would be able to receive, the greater will be our happiness. To achieve this goal God keeps stretching our hearts so that their capacity would increase. This process of stretching can cause pain but this is a beneficial pain, we receive it for our own sake, it comes from God's immense love for us. So, some of the suffering we experience comes from God's working in us, from His activity of stretching our hearts the capacity of which to receive love may have shrunk very small because of our self-centeredness; we should gratefully tolerate this blissful pursuit.

Our personal pain has also cosmic dimensions. In the present stage of God's plan of salvation, evil is still part of the world, and there's a universal war going on between God and the Evil One, and in this war we, humans, are the battlefield. God fights a single combat with Satan for each of us. Since it's impossible for us to stay out of this war and just to sit and wait quietly on the sidewalk for its outcome, in the present economy of salvation attacks of evil, causing suffering, pain, even death, are an unavoidable feature of life: they are necessary part of the human condition. We cannot remain neutral in this war: we have to decide on whose side we will fight, and we make this decision each time when before we do something we choose between good and evil. Our Captain in this war, Jesus Christ, laid down the principle: life can come only out of death. "Unless a grain of wheat falls into the earth and dies, it remains alone; but if it dies, it bears much fruit" (John 12:24). Moral: We're soldiers in the cosmic war between God and Evil in which we cannot avoid pain and sacrifice.

The 20th century great Catholic Hungarian poet, Mihály Babits, was dying in throat cancer. His pain was excruciating. In an advanced stage of his illness, when he no longer was able to speak, he wrote on his note pad: "This must have a reason…" I was trying to shed light on the mystery of suffering from several angles; but at the end we have to realize that suffering and pain are, ultimately, a mystery indeed, never to be understood completely yet to be lived in our daily lives, a mystery of love that never can be fully grasped by the intellect but only by the heart because, as the 17th century French philosopher Blaise Pascal says, "The heart has its reasons which reason itself does not know."

22

EASTER (1)

During the Middle Ages, European towns competed to see which town could build the biggest, tallest, and most magnificent cathedral. Construction of a cathedral could take several decades. Besides the skilled masons and other professional builders, every inhabitant of the town was welcomed to pitch in and work in whatever way he was able to.

In one town the construction had been going on for a long while. The walls were already soaring into the heights when one morning an old man showed up and asked the foreman to assign him some work. He wanted to add his share in building his town's cathedral. Trying to dissuade him, the foreman replied that he was too old and weak to do this kind of work, but the old man insisted that he wanted to help. Finally, to get rid of him, the foreman assigned him a part of the wall inside the church, high, close to the ceiling, under one of the vaults, and the old man set to work happily. From that day on he showed up every morning, climbed up on the scaffolding, and stayed there until sunset. A long while later someone noticed the absence of the old man. The foreman and some workers climbed the scaffolding. At the top they found the old man lying there dead with a happy smile on his face. And on the wall they saw the most beautiful mosaic image of the risen Jesus Christ with the inscription underneath: "He is risen: we shall rise." Our old friend died happily because in his faith he knew that one day he would rise because Jesus Christ rose from the dead.

In the 1960s, as America was preparing to send human beings to the Moon, there was a heated debate in the media about whether or not it was too dangerous to send men to the Moon. After all, we didn't know what the surface there is like; maybe it's such a thick layer of dust that a human would sink in it, as if he were in quicksand. But on the day of July 20, 1969, when we heard on our television sets "the Eagle has landed" and saw Neil Armstrong step on the surface of the Moon, all these debates stopped. Neil Armstrong proved to everyone that it is possible for a human being to walk on the Moon, and, if properly prepared and dressed in the proper space suit, any of us could do it.

It is the same in the case of resurrection. People may have wondered whether the resurrection of human beings is possible or not. For example, at the time of Jesus, Pharisees and Sadducees debated the issue bitterly. Doubting the possibility of resurrection was understandable because it never happened. Christ's resurrection changed all that. If resurrection could take place for one man, it is possible to happen to any and all of us. The old man who died on the scaffold was right: "He is risen: we shall rise!" Actually, we can say that the whole purpose of the work of our salvation was that every human being, liberated from the burden of his sins, would be able to rise into an eternal, glorious life. The Son of God took on a human nature at the event of Incarnation. He lived among us

Chapter 22: Easter (1)

for thirty-three years as a simple human being. Then He suffered torture and died on the cross as a criminal, redeeming all human beings from their sins, and He rose from the dead in a victorious, eternal, glorious body (the Bible calls it a "spiritual body"). It is important to be aware that Jesus rose from the dead for us, for our salvation, for the sake of the human race, not for His own sake. Jesus did not rise just to prove Himself, just to show that He is stronger than Satan and death. Jesus' rising for His own sake would have meant a victory for Satan rather than for God because Jesus would have done exactly what Satan was tempting Him to do in the first place. After all, Satan never denied the power of Jesus to perform miracles. At the temptations of Jesus in the desert, Satan tried to prompt Jesus to perform miracles, but to perform them not for the sake of others but for His own sake, to find satisfaction in His superhuman abilities. But just as with all His other miracles Jesus wanted to help other human beings, He rose from the dead not for Himself but for us, for each of us. In the human nature of Jesus, the whole human race rose to a new, immortal life.

Unfortunately, today the mind of an average person has been shaped more by Hollywood than by the Bible, and thus we are tempted to understand the story of Jesus as a common TV show. In the story line of a usual TV episode, Good and Evil struggle. Although the power of the Good is impressive, for a while Evil seems to be stronger and more cunning. It even looks as though it will ultimately win over the Good, but at the end, after a heroic combat and going through mortal dangers, the Good overcomes its opponent and comes out victorious. The story usually has a happy ending: the good heroes congratulate each other and quickly forget about the whole ordeal, saying, "Thank heaven it's over!"

The Pascal Mystery, the story of Jesus' suffering, death, and resurrection, has a completely different character. Jesus' passion story is not the kind of crisis or ordeal which is to be overcome and then forgotten and left behind. Don't forget that Jesus kept in His risen, glorified body His wounds on His hands and feet and in His side. In a way, exactly these wounds became for Him a kind of ID card: they proved that the risen man is indeed the crucified Jesus of Nazareth. We remember how Jesus spoke to the incredulous apostle Thomas: "Put your finger here and see my hands, and bring your hand and put it into my side, and do not be unbelieving, but believe" (John 20:27). Jesus did not want to make His suffering and death become like a kind of past trial of a great hero but He wanted to incorporate them into the glory of the resurrection. Jesus' sufferings, death, and resurrection together constitute one and the same Pascal Mystery, one and the same set of events that together as <u>one</u> have brought salvation to you, to me, to the whole human race. When Jesus said, "When I am lifted up from the earth, I will draw all people to myself" (John 12:32), He intended to give to this expression of being "lifted up" a double meaning: being lifted up physically on the cross at His crucifixion, and being lifted up from the tomb into the glory of His resurrection. Jesus spoke more than once about His impending sufferings and death as His glorification. After Judas Iscariot left the Upper Room to betray his Master, that is, at the moment when the tragic events of

Chapter 22: Easter (1)

His Passion had just begun, Jesus said, "Now the Son of Man has been glorified and God has been glorified in him" (John 13:31). The two sides, the two halves of the story of Jesus, the sad and the happy, the tragic and the glorious cannot be separated from each other: they form an integral unity, oneness. This is how the Cross, the instrument of execution and death, the instrument of the most painful and worst kind of death became the glorious symbol of our redemption. "He is risen: we shall rise!" This cross, as a glorious sign of victory, appeared to Emperor Constantine in the sky on the evening before his great battle at the Bridge of Milvius in 311 A.D. with the words under it, "*In hoc signo vinces*—In this sign you will be victorious."

We have to realize also that Christ's risen life, our risen life that St. John calls "the eternal life," does not start after our death or on Judgment Day: it started at the time of our baptism when we received a share in Christ's risen life. Christ's Resurrection is already present in us in a hidden way; we carry it in ourselves and it stays with us always unless we expel it from our soul by some serious sinful act. Christ's risen life hidden in us is our real life that can turn even our personal crosses and failures into victory. Jesus said, "I am the resurrection and the life" (John 11:25), meaning also: "I am your resurrection and your life." Christ's risen life hidden in us must penetrate our daily living, must transform our thinking, our speaking and acting. Let's make Christ's resurrection present in our world wherever God's will has placed us: in our families and communities, at our work place, in all the spots where we'll be able to help needy persons, in the sure knowledge that "He is risen: we shall rise!"

23

EASTER (2)

In monasteries, early in the morning, the monks start the Divine Office every day all the year around by the recitation of one of the most beautiful psalms, Psalm 95, which is a joyful invitation to praise God. During Easter time we recite this psalm for forty days; each morning, we repeat seven times the same antiphon, "The Lord is risen, alleluia!" And yet, these words never become boring, obsolete, out of date, or out of place, just like saying "I love you" to a loved one is never boring. These words always maintain the same actuality, the same importance, the same newness for our lives because they articulate the most basic and most important statement of the Christian religion. Without Christ's resurrection there would be for us <u>no salvation, no life, no Church, no sacraments, no joy, no hope</u>. The fact of the resurrection is the rock foundation of our faith. Let's take these points and consider them one by one.

Without Christ's resurrection there would be <u>no salvation</u>. Most people think that we have been redeemed by the sufferings and death of Jesus, which is absolutely true, but it's not the whole and complete truth. Jesus' sufferings and death alone, without the Resurrection, could not and would not have given us salvation. Only one half of His redeeming work, Jesus' passion and death is the downward road, going down into the depth of our common human plight, into the misery of our sinful condition; it is His acceptance of the totality of our human destiny, including its very darkness—pain, suffering, and death—in the worst form possible. Without the Resurrection the redeeming work would be incomplete. In the strict sense of the word, it would be a dark, hopeless "dead end." It would be death without life, failure without victory, darkness without light. As St. Paul writes to the Corinthians, "If Christ has not been raised, your faith is pointless and you have not, after all, been released from your sins" (1 Cor 15:17). Or as he says to the Romans, "If you declare with your heart that Jesus is Lord, and if you believe with your heart that God raised Him from the dead, then you will be saved" (Rom 10:9). In the letter to the Ephesians, we read "God through the great love with which he loved us, even when we were dead in our sins, brought us to life with Christ, and raised us up with him and gave us a place with him in heaven, in Christ Jesus" (Eph 2:4-6). Yes, it's the resurrection of Jesus that completes the work of salvation. The resurrection is the upward road, the victory of life and light over death and darkness, Christ's ultimate victory over sin. It's a wonderful exchange: becoming a human being Jesus obtained the ability to suffer and to die, and He as God gives us the ability to rise to a new life and live—to live not only 60 or 80 or 100 years but to live forever in union with God. Christ's death and resurrection <u>together</u>, as a whole, are called the "Paschal Mystery." And this is why we love to remind ourselves, "The Lord is risen, alleluia!"

Chapter 23: Easter (2)

Without resurrection there would be <u>no life</u>. Jesus never said, "I am the death," but He did say, "I am the way, the truth, and the life" (John 14:6). He also said, "I am the resurrection and the life" (John 10:10). On Easter morning when the women arrived at the tomb, the two angels said to them, "Why do you seek the living one among the dead? He is not here, but He has been raised" (Luke 24:5-6). Jesus, who is called in the Acts of the Apostles the Author of Life, <u>is</u> Life Himself. The purpose of his coming is to <u>give</u> His life to us: He said, "I have come so that they may have life, and have it to the full" (John 10:10). By His death and resurrection, He defeated death itself; His death and resurrection together caused the death of death itself. Yes, because He is risen, we shall also rise. By rising from the dead Himself, He gave us the possibility, even the ability that we, too, by God's power, should rise to a new, incorruptible, eternal life. This life is not just some kind of a waiting for an uncertain future. We who believe in Jesus and try to follow Him already have this eternal life within us now, here on earth. God's eternal life is within us and wants to be shown, to be expressed, to be made visible in and through our everyday lives. And what exactly is this eternal life? It is the divine life, God's immortal, unlimited life within our mortal, limited bodies, the tremendous, unfathomable life of the Holy Trinity cascading between the Father and the Son and the Holy Spirit unceasingly for all eternity, the eternal life which we call in the language of theology sanctifying grace. We have all the reasons to never stop boasting and proclaiming the ultimate good news of Jesus: "The Lord is risen, alleluia!"

Without resurrection there would be <u>no Church</u>. Without Jesus' resurrection, there would be no Christian community, no togetherness, no unity possible. After Jesus died, his disciples were scattered physically and emotionally. They fled, they split up, they went home, they retreated into their loneliness, into their isolation. Without Christ's Resurrection, that would have been the final state of things: Jesus would have been just a short period of light of brotherhood and companionship in the immense, ice-cold, lonely darkness of world history, and after His death, that light would have been extinguished forever. Just think of the sad conversation of the disciples of Emmaus before the risen Jesus joined them (Luke 23:13-14). But it did not happen that way. Jesus promised, "When I am lifted up from the earth, I will draw everyone to myself" (John 12:32). The expression "lifted up" has at the same time a double meaning: the lifting up of Jesus on the wood of the cross and His being lifted up high in the glory of His resurrection and ascension. His death and resurrection <u>together</u> accomplish this magnetic effect. His resurrection worked like a magnet at the first Pentecost and drew together the first Christian community and gave life to the Church. This magnet has been working ever since for two thousand years; in every age, on every continent new generations of people keep joining the flock of Jesus the Good Shepherd. This is also a magnificent reason why we keep repeating, "The Lord is risen, alleluia!"

Without resurrection there would be <u>no sacraments</u>. It is the power of Jesus' resurrection that works in each sacrament and bestows upon each its life-giving vigor. It is through the sacraments

Chapter 23: Easter (2)

that Jesus' risen life, the life of the Holy Trinity, enters our little, fragile, human life. Baptism is so closely connected with the resurrection that it is conferred most properly during the Easter Vigil ceremony. The newly baptized person rises to new life in Christ. The sacrament of penance was given to the apostles on the day of Jesus' resurrection, during His first appearance to them, showing in this way, that the resurrection made it possible for this power to be passed on to His followers. The handing on of this sacrament was so urgent that Jesus did not want to wait even one more day. In the Holy Eucharist, it is the Body and Blood of the <u>risen</u> Jesus we receive; it is the entire Paschal Mystery—the suffering, death, and resurrection—that becomes present at each celebration of the Mass. And in all the other sacraments it's the risen Christ who is at work, who is continuing to do within the Church His healing, comforting, forgiving, strengthening, life-giving activity that He did during His public ministry in Judea and Galilee. This is why we keep reminding ourselves, "The Lord is risen, alleluia!"

If without resurrection we could not have salvation and life, the Church and the sacraments, then we <u>could not have joy and hope</u> in our lives either. Without the risen Jesus, our life would be utterly hopeless, joyless, and purposeless. All our joy is Easter joy, and all our hope is Easter hope. Hope is always directed toward a brighter future. If the death of Jesus had been the end, no matter how heroic and generous His self-sacrifice was, there would be no future and no hope for us. But Jesus is indeed risen, and by His resurrection, He gives us joy. Look at the disciples on Easter Sunday: after the sadness and darkness and despair of Friday and Saturday, now they're filled with unrestrainable joy. They run to the tomb, they run to the upper room, the disciples of Emmaus run their marathon back to Jerusalem, everyone is excited, everyone is breathless. They just cannot contain their joy. This same indomitable joy runs through the twenty Christian centuries, and the hope of this new life animates every Christian in every age. The promise of this new life gives meaning to our lives: as we read on the last page of the Bible, "God will make his home among them, they will be his people, and he will be their God, and God will be with them. He will wipe away all tears from their eyes, there will be no more death, and no more mourning or sadness or pain. The world of the past has gone" (Rev 21:3-4). This is the reason why we keep announcing to each other the joyful news, "The Lord is risen, Alleluia!"

24

PEACE

"Blessed are the peacemakers, for they shall be called children of God" (Mt 5:9). Jesus Christ who proclaimed these words—the Son of God by nature, not just by adoption—is our Peacemaker, <u>the</u> Peacemaker. But to gain peace for us, Christ had to wage a war. It's undeniable, and we're all witnesses to it, that there is a constant war going on in the universe: a war between good and evil, between life and death, between light and darkness, between God and Satan. In this war, right at the dawn of mankind's history, Satan lured woman and man to his side. The human being rebelled against God: he wanted to make himself his own "god" and, as a result, he lost his peace for good. After a number of unsuccessful attempts on the part of God to restore the original peace—after several failed covenants, broken promises, frustrated plans—Jesus Christ was the one who, at last, as a true High Priest (*Pontifex* = Bridge-builder), rebuilt the bridge between the Creator and His creatures, reestablished the ultimate peace between God and man, and repaired the damage that sin had made on God's plan of salvation. The final combat between God and Satan was won by God on Calvary Hill when Jesus Christ died on the Cross and, three days later, when He rose from the dead. Now, in the joy of Easter, this peace is being offered to each human being within Christ's Church. The question is: Do you have this peace?

The "password" in the Benedictine life-style is PAX, Peace. Above the entrance of many monasteries, we can see this sign: PAX. Every monastery is supposed to be an island of peace in a world that is ravaged by dissent, contention, war, and violence; every Christian is supposed to be a solid rock of peace in the stormy sea.

In the early twentieth century, Hungarian author Margit Kafka wrote a novel about the life of nuns living in a convent. She gave her book the title *Ant-hill* because the story was the chronicle of an endless series of intrigues, feuds, and pitiable hatreds that made life in that community miserable. We can ask ourselves the question: What are we building within ourselves as a person and within our environment: peace or an ant-hill?

What is peace? I never liked very much the scholastic definition of peace: *Tranquillitas ordinis*, tranquility, stillness, restfulness of order. This sounds to me a formula that is too negative: absence of movement – almost suggesting the idea of the absence of life. Peace must be much more than that. What did Jesus say? "Peace I leave with you; my peace I give to you; not as the world gives do I give it to you" (John 14:27). In three steps, Jesus builds up the idea of what true peace is: (1) He's giving peace to His friends, not just as the absence of wars and conflicts but as something positive, full of life, as His special gift, as His inheritance, as His legacy; (2) He points out that this will be His peace, indicating that there are two different kinds of peace; (3) the peace that Jesus gives is totally different from the peace that the world can provide.

The world is unable to give true peace: what the world gives is always just an appearance of peace, a fake peace, a lie. The world does not know real peace. Shortly before His suffering, Jesus wept over the future destiny of the holy city Jerusalem (the common interpretation of the name of Jerusalem is "City of Peace"!) that was about to convict and crucify Him, and said: "If this day you only knew what makes for peace – but now it is hidden from your eyes" (Lk 19:42). The peace of the world only appears to be peace; yes, it's quiet and silent on the surface but this surface is a very thin layer of solid ground and underneath the lava is boiling with the constant threat of a volcanic eruption at any instant. On the surface maybe there is peace: the peace of death, a frozen stillness imposed by fear. It is the peace of a battlefield after the fighting is over and dead bodies cover the ground. It is the peace of Hiroshima after the explosion of the Bomb. It is the peace of Auschwitz and of the Gulag; the peace of barbed wire fences, and guard towers, and machine guns aimed at you. It is the peace of cemeteries, the peace of death. As Jeremiah writes, they say, "Peace, peace, when there is no peace" (Jer 6:14).

This is the peace of Holy Saturday, the peace of that sad Saturday following the darkness of Good Friday when seemingly all hope was gone, when it seemed that the world of evil had won, when that "troublemaker" Rabbi from Galilee was done away with for good, executed and securely buried in a sealed tomb; at last His words would not disturb any longer the ears of the Pharisees and the high priests. The peace that the world gives is the peace of the absence of Jesus. And what happened to the disciples on that day? They indeed lost their hope. They got scared and scattered; they were isolated, were left alone with their fears and their sadness. Yes, the peace that the world can give results in hopelessness and fear.

The true peace is the peace of Christ, *Pax Christi*. It is the peace that is gushing forth from the loving Trinitarian union of Father, Son, and Holy Spirit. It is the peace of unshakable harmony and love—the peace that Jesus brought on earth, the peace that Jesus conquered for us and sealed by shedding His own blood as the high price of our true peace. The peace of Christ is the peace of Easter morning, the peace of resurrection. And this peace is anything but stillness and quiet. The first Easter morning was filled with excitement and joy, with running and carrying messages; it was filled with unexpected, mysterious encounters, yet it was exuberant peace. The peace of Jesus is not the absence of something (like the absence of movement) but rather throbbing life, bursting energy, new birth, new creation, continuous growth. It's not a still pond but an abundant spring, a rushing creek, a roaring waterfall; it's not frozen immobility but rather a bursting superabundance. The peace of Christ is the peace of Niagara Falls.

When Jesus first came to the apostles after His resurrection, He greeted them in the usual Jewish custom, "Peace be with you!" But this time the traditional greeting was much more than the usual "Shalom!" This time "Peace" was Jesus' first word to His disciples after His resurrection because peace was the great gift of

Easter; it was the fulfillment of the angels' Christmas song, "Glory to God in the highest and peace on earth to men of good will." Jesus' greeting of peace was not a call for stillness: the greeting was immediately connected with the order of becoming active, of starting to do things, of going to other people. Listen to Jesus speak, "Peace be with you. As the Father has sent me, even so <u>I send you</u>" (John 20:21). Then He breathed on them and said, "Receive the Holy Spirit!" (John 20:22). Jesus' peace reaches us through the presence of the Holy Spirit. The Holy Spirit is the holy wind that is blowing us toward other men and women with a joyful message, like the wind blowing the "parachutes" of the tiny seeds of a dandelion far away. The Holy Spirit makes us partners of Jesus in bringing into our environment the fresh air of peace. As He was sent to us by the Father, He's sending us to other people.

What is the person of peace like? The man of peace is joyful and serene, optimistic; he makes bold projects as he looks into the future with hope. Someone said that the person whose plans outweigh his memories remains always young. The person of peace remains always young. Initial lack of success, even failures, don't stop him from trying again because he knows that from the greatest failure ever, Christ's death on the cross, issued the greatest victory, Christ's resurrection. He knows that the tree of failure, the cross, ultimately became the new Tree of Life in the center of the new Garden of Eden of the new creation. The person of peace is able to start again from scratch because in spirit he has grown above the clouds of worries and troubles, above the clouds where there is always sunshine. He does not lose courage because he knows that "everything works for the good of those who love God" (Rom 8:28). The person of peace is an individual of indomitable hope because he or she can see everywhere, in every person, in every situation the promise of new life, the promise of the resurrection.

25

BLACK HOLE

This will be a strange, modern-day parable. Let's start. The kingdom of heaven is like a black hole. Like all creatures, stars also have a life history. New stars are born, and then they become young, middle-aged, and old. Finally, stars die. A black hole is the last stage of the existence of a star. It is actually a "deceased" or dead star in its extinguished, collapsed, shrunken state. Jesus Christ, sent to mankind in the "last times," has several features similar to a black hole.

1. The black hole is very <u>small</u>. Our sun is about one million times bigger than the earth, but it is considered by astronomers to be quite a small star compared to those that are hundreds or thousands of times bigger than our sun. Yet, in its collapsed state the mass of a big star becomes very small. There are three common types of black holes. We talk about the smallest one, called a stellar black hole, which forms after a giant star explodes and collapses on itself; it is estimated that it measures not more than about forty miles across, roughly three times the length of Manhattan. In His great love for us human beings, God, the almighty, unlimited Creator of the universe, unlimited in

every way, became very small, became a tiny, helpless, weak newborn baby. The immortal God became mortal, the all-powerful became powerless, and the inviolable became vulnerable. God "shrank," became very small, like a stellar black hole.

It is one of love's rules that the one who loves wishes to be similar to his loved one. Well, how could we complain about our pains and troubles with trust in a God who, in His absolute perfection and happiness, would not know what suffering is? But Jesus—in whom God became very small, small like us human beings—became "one of us." To Him we can turn with confidence in all our troubles because He went through the same crises—and even more.
Another rule of love is that its basic tendency is "toward union." One who loves wishes to become united with his beloved. This second rule impelled Jesus to become even smaller, to shrink even more: to reduce Himself into a morsel of bread, into a drop of wine, so that as food and drink He could be completely one with those whom He loved. The One whose bread was to do always the will of His Father, by the will of His Father became Himself bread. Are these features of God not a call also for us to become small, to give up our imagined "greatness," to become bread for others to be distributed and consumed?

2. A black hole is total <u>blackness,</u> a dark hole in space. Yes, because its gravitation is so strong that not even light can

escape from it; it is completely dark. The trouble with us people is not so much that we are small: the trouble is that we're black, black and ugly from sin. We live in the darkness of sin. But no matter how unlovable we are in that condition, God loved us so much that He, the Light, came into our darkness. "The light shines in the darkness and the darkness has not overcome it" (Jn 1:5). He not only came into the darkness but became darkness, became sin in order to destroy sin by His own death: "For our sake He [God] made Him [Christ] to be sin who did not know sin so that we might become the righteousness of God in Him" (2 Cor 5:21). Christ, the Light of the world, took on Himself the blackness and darkness of our sins. In the Incarnation Christ's humanity hid His divinity. In His act of redemption, his suffering and death hid even the beauty of His humanity: "I am a worm, not a human, scorned by everyone, despised by the people" (Ps 22:7); and "God [...] having forgiven us all our trespasses, having canceled the bond [the record of our sins] which stood against us with its legal demands: this he set aside, nailing it to the cross" (Col 2:14-15).

3. The black hole is totally black because of its tremendous power of gravity: it's so small but it has all the matter that the huge sun had but in a collapsed state and so it has the same gravitational force. It's black because it attracts and swallows up all the light; it cannot emit and reflect it. Jesus

Christ has the same kind of gravitational force. He irresistibly attracts people. Just take the stories of the apostles: Jesus' one word drew them to Him. Peter, Andrew, John, James, Matthew, and later Paul followed Jesus after His first call. Think of the myriads of saints who answered Christ's call on the "narrow way." He expressed this quality of His several times: "When I am lifted up from the earth, I will draw all men to myself" (Jn 12:32). Jesus calls, "Come to me all who labor and are heavily laden, and I will give you rest" (Mt 11:28); "If anyone thirsts, let him come to me and drink" (Jn 7:37); "I am the bread of life: he who comes to me shall not hunger" (Jn 6:35); "where two or three are gathered in my name, there am I in the midst of them" (Mt 18:20). Later on, Jesus speaks in the name of His Father: "How often would I have gathered your children together as a hen gathers her brood under her wings, and you would not" (Mt 23:37). "Many will come from east and west and sit at table with Abraham, Isaac, and Jacob in the kingdom of heaven" (Mt 8:11). But this "attraction" or "gravitation" will really work only after the "hour" of Jesus: "When I am lifted up...."

4. Astronomers say that the black <u>hole</u> is a hole not only in space but also <u>in time</u>: if it were possible to pass through it, one would fall into a completely different time categpry, in a different eon. The gospel of Jesus is the "good news" because the last word of His story was said not on Calvary

Hill but at the empty tomb: *"Et resurrexit tertia die."* Jesus came into our darkness and He himself became darkness to take us out of this darkness and take us over into the light and splendor of God. The passage into God's light is Jesus' resurrection. It was revealed in His resurrection that the tiny Baby of Bethlehem was in fact the immeasurable almighty God; that the bloody, sweaty, muddy face of the crucified Jesus was the face of the glorious Lord. In Jesus' resurrection it was revealed that God's love is a strong love, stronger than anything else in the world, certainly stronger than evil and sin and death. Salvation History is a passage of time of many millennia and we, people living in the twenty-first century, are an integral part of that history. Jesus' coming, suffering, death, and resurrection completed this history, and with that completion, we entered, as the beginning of the letter to the Hebrews states, into the "last days." We are living now in the end times, in a different quality of time, in a time which already is touching eternity. We are living in the time of the *Parousia*, approaching the Final Day, getting closer every day to the Second Coming of the Lord.

26

ASCENSION

Forty days after Easter Sunday, the Church celebrates and rejoices in the mystery of the Ascension, the rising of our Lord into the glory of God, His Father. But are we really rejoicing? Do we have any reason for rejoicing? Do we experience joy, or rather sadness? I remember a remark that I read in the spiritual diary of a saintly nun: "Ascension," she wrote, "the saddest day of the year because Jesus is leaving us." Is the solemnity of Ascension really the saddest feast of the year? Logically, the question can rise in our hearts: If Jesus loves us, why would He leave us?

One thing we have to state strongly and for sure: Man can leave God by sinning but God will never leave man. Jesus never leaves us. As long as man remains faithfully in a loving relationship with God, God will be always present to man. God remains close even to a sinful man, waiting for his conversion, like the father of the prodigal son. This is a fact.

But there are different kinds of presences. A human personality has a great number of different facets like a diamond; it can have a wealth of different shades caused by different moods, different situations, by changes in age, in health, even in temperament. In a similar way, a person can be present to another person in a great variety of ways. God's "personality" has an infinite number of facets, an infinite wealth of varieties, and so does the way He is able to be present to us. The whole of eternity would not be enough to unfold all these possibilities. The name *Yahweh* means not only "He who <u>is</u>," but also "He who is <u>with us</u>." *Yahweh* is also *Emmanuel,* "God-with-us," the God who remains always present, but in a great variety of ways.

God is for us as the sun is for the earth. The sun is always present to planet earth. The earth always remains in the orbit of the sun, but the sun is present to it in a constantly changing way as the globe turns, changing during the hours of the day. Night follows the day, and as the months pass one season follows the other. God's "comings" and "leavings" are nothing else than such changes in the manner of His presence. The sun is present to our planet in the brightness of noon, in the orange glow of the sunset, even in the darkness of night. As life is never static and immovable, so God's presence to us is changing all the time. The Father was united with Jesus even on the cross when He cried out, "God, my God, why have you forsaken me?" (Mt 27:46). The Father was present at the hour of Jesus' Transfiguration and on Easter morning with the Apostles. But God is present to us also in our agonies and struggles when we don't perceive His tender touch in our lives. All this means that Jesus remains present to us even when He seemingly "leaves" this world in His Ascension—after all, He Himself said, "I will not leave you orphans" (John 14:18). Through the events of the Ascension and later at Pentecost, His visible, outward presence to His Apostles changed into an inner, invisible presence through the coming of the Holy Spirit. From "outside" of them He came "inside" of them into a presence in faith and sacrament, which, in a way, was more real and more powerful than His bodily presence ever had been before. Jesus said to doubting Thomas, "You have come to believe because you have seen me. Happy are those who do not see, yet believe" (John 20:29). Such changes in the forms of the presence of Jesus, His manifold ways of coming, add beauty and variety to our togetherness with Him, even when they can also be tests of our faithfulness, making us stronger and more resilient. We are constantly enriched by these different experiences of God's presence. By the degree of our devotedness, we can always grow in the intensity of our love and dedication to the Lord, in our experience of God's presence.

In daily Christian life we struggle to try to live every moment of our days in His presence. We strive to allow this presence to penetrate our entire existence so that every crevice and nook of our souls will be filled with this divine presence, this *shekinah*, just as it was in the Meeting Tent in the desert. Our souls should be places like the Upper Room, or the room in Emmaus, or the home of Martha in Bethany where the Lord is welcomed, where He can lodge and make His home with us. We have to carry on with our lives. We have to bear with courage the different experiences of God's presence, even those that take the appearance of an absence, but we should know that no matter what we feel, we're with Him in the Upper Room, reclining our heads on His chest, at perfect peace.

The Ascension is just one phase in the entire journey of Jesus, the most glorious phase at that! To appreciate it correctly, we have to place it in the context of the entire journey, just as St. Paul writes it in his letter to the Philippians (2:6-11). We know well the text: "Though he was in the form of God…." The Son of God comes down from heaven diving like a meteor in the night sky or like a roller coaster in an amusement park, down into the depth of the greatest misery of human existence, even into death, dying as a convicted criminal on the cross. But at this deepest point the direction changes. He's going up into the glory of Resurrection and Ascension, back to His Father in heaven. At the deepest point the meteor changes direction and soars up into heaven. Christ came down in His divinity, taking up His divinity <u>and</u> humanity. Yet, with His Ascension He takes along not just humanity in general. In a concrete way, He takes His human nature into the glory of God, even including the wounds on His body, the marks of His suffering. Even more than that, He takes up with Him His brothers and sisters. The meteor now becomes a comet and the risen Christ goes up not alone but drawing behind Him, like the tail of the comet, all His faithful disciples whom He has made His brothers and sisters. "He ascended on high and took prisoners captive" (Eph 4:8; cf. Ps 68:19). Together they go up to the Father because Christ and the Church are one, and the body cannot be separated from the Head.

During His earthly life, Jesus of Nazareth was seen and heard in a very limited time only by very few (maybe just a few thousand)

Chapter 26: Ascension

people in a faraway corner of the Roman Empire. But as the incarnate Son of God, He came on earth to be seen and heard by every human being in every age and every country. Ascension means that Jesus is coming to every man and woman no matter when and where they lived: He wants to encounter them all. The lamp on my desk sheds a small circle of light. If I lift up the lamp, the circle becomes larger. As I lift the source of light higher and higher, the circle of light becomes larger and larger. If man launches a satellite into the space, the "tent" of that object could cover on earth one or more continents, even the whole sphere of the planet. This circle of light can be understood as Jesus' presence in the world. Jesus said, "I am the light of the world" (John 8:12). We can understand the image of Ascension also in this way: Jesus, "the light of the world," ascending into heaven, is not leaving us but, while remaining with us, He just expands His presence (and keeps expanding it) to other people, to other nations, to people all over the world.

After Jesus went up to heaven and a cloud covered Him from the apostles' eyes, an angel appeared and asked them, "Men of Galilee, why are you standing there looking at the sky?" (Acts 1:11). It was as if he were saying, "Don't just look at the sky idle: you have a big job to do! Go and make disciples of all the nations, baptizing them and teaching them to observe all that Jesus has commanded you." It is St. Paul who warns us, "If you were raised with Christ, seek what is above, where Christ is seated at the right hand of God. Think of what is above, not of what is on earth" (Col 3:1-2). We Christians have two home countries: one is here on earth and the other is above in heaven. We are citizens of both countries: we are at home in both lands. Our two feet are solidly planted on earth, but our head is already in heaven. Here on earth we have to work with all our efforts to build the Kingdom of God; but at the same time in our minds we are already at home in heaven with the Lord. Here on earth we struggle and labor and shed the sweat of our brows, but with our spirit we are already peacefully contemplating the Lord in heaven. The mystery of Ascension does not separate us from the Lord, but rather it connects heaven and earth because one of us, Jesus Christ, a true human being, is already up there interceding for us with the Father.

27

HOLY SPIRIT

Who is the Holy Spirit?

Preachers like to call the Holy Spirit the "unknown God." Indeed, for God the Father we may have a mental picture as a powerful father figure, just as Jesus did call Him Father, or "Abba," "Dear Father," almost the equivalent of the English word "Daddy." Or as Michelangelo painted Him on the ceiling of the Sistine Chapel. We also can picture God the Son as the good Galilean rabbi teaching and performing miracles, or as the crucified Savior, or the glorious risen *Pantocrator*. But we don't have any biblical help to imagine the Holy Spirit. At the baptism of Jesus, the Holy Spirit appeared as a dove, maybe reminding us of Noah's dove with an olive branch in her beak as the symbol of peace, or recalling the turtledove of the Song of Songs symbolizing the "Beloved." But we know that the Holy Spirit is not a bird. What image can we have of the Holy Spirit?

In ancient Greece, millennia before the Russian scientist D. I. Mendeleev during the 1860s developed the periodic table classifying the elements, the general view was that the world is composed of four elements: air, fire, water, and earth (plain soil). Meditating on the mystery of the Holy Spirit, we discover that biblical thought applies these four elements to the Holy Spirit and the Church, and that the metaphors are used with particular force in the story of the first Pentecost.

1. <u>The Holy Spirit is air moving as blowing wind.</u>

For people of ancient times, with more poetic insight than scientific knowledge, the wind, the movement of the air, was felt as a mysterious power, a divine element. We know that the wind is here yet we cannot see it; what we see is only the effect caused by the wind: trees swaying, flags fluttering, and dry leaves flying in the air. We don't know where the wind is coming from or where it is going. At one time, the wind may be a gentle breeze; at another, a destructive hurricane or tornado.

We read at the very beginning of the Old Testament in the first verses of the first chapter of Genesis: "In the beginning, when God created the heavens and the earth, the earth was a formless wasteland and darkness covered the abyss, while a mighty wind swept over the waters" (1:1-2). What is this formless wasteland, what is this wind, what are these waters? It is the primordial chaos over which the mighty wind, God's powerful breath, is hovering. In the Hebrew language, two phenomena, wind and human breath, were denoted by the same noun, *ruah*, and the wind was understood as the breath of God. In corners of ancient maps, we can see a human face blowing the wind. Just like at the creation of the universe, a strong wind, God's divine breath, was hovering over the waters. At the creation of man, God breathed His divine breath of life into

Chapter 27: Holy Spirit

the nostrils of Adam, causing this man, a sculpture made of clay, to become alive (Gen 2:7). At the time of Exodus, God saved His people by drying up the sea with a mighty wind that blew all night long (Ex 14:21). On Mount Sinai, Elijah experienced God's presence in a gentle breeze (1 Kings 19:11-12).

When the "fullness of time" arrived, Jesus, talking to Nicodemus, connected the Holy Spirit with the idea of wind. He said, "The wind blows where it wills, and you can hear the sound it makes, but you do not know where it comes from or where it goes; so it is with everyone who is born of the Spirit" (John 3:8). On the day when Jesus rose from the dead and appeared to the apostles the first time, he greeted them by saying, "Peace be with you," and he breathed on them, just as the Creator breathed into the nostrils of Adam and said, "Receive the Holy Spirit." Again, we see the Holy Spirit as the Divine Breath.

Given such biblical precedents, on the day of Pentecost, when the apostles heard the sound of a strong wind, they must have realized that this wind meant an epiphany, a divine manifestation; that it was the powerful sign of the descent of the Holy Spirit on them, just as Jesus had promised (see Acts 1:8; 2:2). The wind that the apostles experienced the first time in the Upper Room was later indeed blowing them in every direction on earth to proclaim the gospel to the ends of the earth.

2. <u>The Holy Spirit is fire.</u>

The other visible sign of the coming of the Holy Spirit at Pentecost was the tongues of fire descending on the heads of the apostles. Fire was another mysterious reality for people of ancient times. They could see and feel its presence, yet it was not a touchable solid or liquid. It was perceived as something spiritual. Like wind, fire also could be gentle and useful by providing light, warming homes, and cooking meals. But it could be also a horrible destructive power that mercilessly consumed in a conflagration everything flammable in its way. Fire was also considered an element of heavenly origin, since in ancient times the most powerful fire was lightning and for millennia the only way for man to obtain fire was to separate it from burning wood hit by lightning. We remember that Abraham and Isaac had to carry the fire for the sacrifice (see Gen 22:6). In Greek mythology Prometheus had to steal fire from the gods so that humans might be able to use it.

In the Old Testament, fire was used a number of times as a visible sign of divine presence. When He sealed his covenant with Abraham, God moved through the aisle between the dead animals in the form of fire. God spoke to Moses from a burning bush (Gen 15:17). In Exodus, at night a column of fire led God's people in the desert. The prophet Elijah was taken up into heaven by a chariot of fire.

At the time of the Incarnation of God's Son, Jesus announced His vocation as the start of a fire in our world. He said, "I have come to set the earth on fire, and how I wish it were already blazing!" (Lk 12:49). The letter to the Hebrews states that "our God is a consuming fire" (12:29). This fire is the Holy Spirit. John the Baptist announced that the One who is coming after him "will baptize you with the Holy Spirit and fire" (Mt 3:11).

At the first Pentecost, we see the immediate result of this fire of the Holy Spirit on the apostles: all their fear is suddenly vanished, they're filled with courage and enthusiasm, they open the door of the house, go out among the people and proclaim to the crowd the gospel with such fire that many in the audience think that they're drunk with wine. The miracle of Pentecost was that everybody heard the apostles speaking their mother tongue, a miracle of communication. "They were all astounded and bewildered, and said to one another, 'What does this mean?' But others said, scoffing, 'They have had too much new wine' " (Acts 2:12-13). Peter explained to them what was happening: "These people are not drunk, as you suppose, for it is only nine o'clock in the morning. No, this is what was spoken through the prophet Joel: 'It will come to pass in the last days, God says, that I will pour out a portion of my Spirit upon all flesh. Your sons and daughters will prophesy' " (Acts 2:15-17).

St. Paul reminds us that the fire of the Holy Spirit should have the same effect on us not just momentarily but in a lasting manner: "Do not quench the Spirit," he says (1 Thess 5:19). The same program has been set before us by the great Cistercian saint, St. Bernard of Clairvaux, in his motto: "*Ardere et lucere perfectum*: To enkindle and to enlighten is perfection." The fire of the Holy

Spirit should be kept burning in our hearts so that we can give light and warmth also to other people.

3. The Holy Spirit is water.

In the arid biblical lands one of the main concerns of the people was to have enough fresh water for drinking and washing. They called the fresh running water "living water," as opposed to the stale water of the cisterns. Jesus Christ came to bring the life-giving waters just as God promised it in Isaiah: "I put water in the desert and rivers in the wasteland for my chosen people to drink; I will pour out water upon the thirsty ground, and streams upon the dry land; I will pour out my Spirit upon your offspring" (Isaiah 43:20; 44:3). At Jacob's well Jesus tells the Samaritan woman, "Whoever drinks the water I shall give will never thirst; the water I shall give will become in him a spring of water welling up to eternal life" (John 4:14). We know that "eternal life" in St. John's writings means not simply "life after death," but the life of God, the sanctifying grace that Christ's disciples receive already here on earth through faith and the sacraments. Baptized Christians have "eternal life" here on earth if they did not lose it by committing serious sins. That these life-giving waters are the Holy Spirit is made clear by a later event. During the feast of booths while he was in the Temple, Jesus called people to Himself: "Let everyone who thirsts come to me and drink. Whoever believes in me, as the Scripture says, rivers of living waters will flow within him." To these words of the Lord the evangelist John adds this comment: "He said this in reference to the Spirit that those who came to believe in Him were to receive" (John 7:37-39). When Jesus dies on the cross, John makes this observation: "One of the soldiers thrust his lance into His side, and immediately blood and water flowed out." John considered this detail important enough to add the remark signifying that he was present when this took place: "An eyewitness has testified, and his testimony is true" (John 19:34-35). The blood and water symbolize the two principal sacraments: the blood of Holy Eucharist and water of baptism. As St. Paul says, Christ is the Rock: "They [the Old Testament Hebrews] all drank the same spiritual drink, for they drank from a spiritual rock that followed them, and the rock was the Christ" (1 Cor 10:4). When this Rock was struck (pierced) it yielded from His side waters enabling men to quench their thirst as they were walking toward the true Promised Land. These waters are nothing else than the Holy Spirit, the life-giving power of God, given by baptism. Regarding the consummation of all things, this living water symbolizes the endless happiness of the elect: "For the Lamb who is in the center of the throne will shepherd them and lead them to springs of life-giving water, and God will wipe away every tear from their eyes" (Rev 7:17). He will say, "I am the Alpha and the Omega, the beginning and the end. To the thirsty, I will give a gift from the spring of life-giving water" (Rev 21:6).

At Jacob's well, Jesus said to the woman, "Whoever drinks the water I shall give will never thirst; the water I shall give will become in him a spring of water welling up to eternal life" (John 4:14). Why does Jesus call "water" the gift of the Holy Spirit? Because every living thing needs water; whatever is alive and is growing consists of water; every tree, and all plants and animals are partly made up of water; no living being can exist without water. Water is always the same, yet the variety of living things is infinite. Out of the same water grow the oak tree and the maple tree. Every living creature uses the same water according to its own requirement. In the same way, the grace of the Holy Spirit is always the same, yet the same grace manifests itself in a seemingly infinite way in every human being. Saint Paul speaks about the Church as the body of Christ. The Holy Spirit is the same, yet the gifts have an infinite variety. St. Paul says, "For in one Spirit we were all baptized into one body, whether Jews or Greeks, slaves or free persons, and we were all given to drink of one Spirit" (1 Cor 12:13). Just as the needs of the Church community are manifold, the gifts given to the community are also manifold. Out of the great variety of people and their great variety of talents and gifts, the Church is formed as one coherent family of people. A few lines later, Paul continues: "Now you are Christ's body, and individually parts of it. Some people God has designated in the Church to be, first, apostles; second, prophets; third, teachers; then, mighty deeds; then gifts of healing, assistance, administration, and varieties of tongues" (1 Cor 12:27-28). Everybody has to contribute to the whole of community by his or her special talents. As each person adds a special personal shade of color, the result becomes a community with the beauty of a rainbow.

4. The fourth element: earth.

Now that we've seen how three of the four elements, which made up the world according to the ancient Greeks, could be applied to the Holy Spirit, what can we say about the fourth element, the earth?

Our mother Church is the fourth element, the earth. The Church was born at the first Pentecost from the power of the Holy Spirit, uniting those who believed in Jesus into one body and constantly animating and making them fruitful. The earth is our Church community, both the local and the universal Church, the mystical body of Christ, the people of God, the community of brothers and sisters made God's children by the redemptive death and resurrection of Jesus Christ and given constantly new life by all the sacraments, but foremost by baptism and the Holy Eucharist.

In Greek mythology Antaeus was a giant, one of the children of Gaea, the goddess Mother Earth. The giant Antaeus was invincible because whenever he touched the earth he regained his strength from his mother, Earth. Antaeus would challenge all passersby to wrestling matches, kill them, and collect their skulls so that from them he might one day build a temple to his father, Poseidon. He was invincibly strong as long as he remained in contact with the earth (that is, with Gaea, his mother), but once lifted into the air he became as weak as other men. Antaeus had defeated most of his opponents until he challenged Hercules. Upon finding out that he could not beat Antaeus by throwing him to the ground since this only restored his strength, Hercules held Antaeus aloft in the air, crushed him in a bear-hug, and thus killed him.

The story of Antaeus can be used as a parable for spiritual warfare. As long as we are spiritually united with our mother Church, we are invincible. But as soon as we lose contact with mother Church, our strength fades away; we become so weak that we will be easily defeated. "*Vae soli!*—Woe to the solitary man!" states King Solomon (Eccl 4:10).

Yes, the Holy Spirit is our environment, our habitat, our atmosphere. The Holy Spirit is the air that we breathe, the fire that animates us, firing us up with enthusiasm and passion, and the water that cleanses us in baptism and quenches our thirst for God. And by the power of the same Holy Spirit, the mother Church, our mother earth, is the solid ground on which we "live and move and have our being" (Acts 17:28), our source of energy and vitality, the mother with whom we must be always connected because as soon as we are separated from her, we lose our strength, we become weak, and we perish.

How did the Holy Spirit come on the apostles?

To talk about the coming of the Holy Spirit at the first Pentecost, we have to start with the mystery of the Ascension. At Ascension, by entering into His eternal glory, Jesus seemingly is leaving His apostles. But what seems to be a leaving is actually a coming closer to His disciples. Jesus is always our merciful Redeemer, our good Shepherd, our intimate Friend. Even if He is seemingly leaving, Jesus actually is always coming; He would never leave us. The event of the Ascension is Jesus' leaving the apostles in one way, so that He would be able to come to them in another even more wonderful and more intimate way. He's leaving the apostles in His visible, bodily form in which He was close to them but always only <u>outside</u> of them. There was still a distance, a separating space, between Him and His disciples. By the Ascension Jesus wants to come <u>inside</u> them to be completely united with them. Also, continuing His visible, bodily presence necessarily would have limited His presence to a very small number of people, and the millions and millions of people to whom Jesus also wanted to be close would have been excluded from the joy of being with Him. So, Jesus wanted to remedy this double limitation on His presence with us. This remedy took place on the day of Pentecost. By sending the Holy Spirit, Jesus gave us a universal, unlimited presence, a presence not limited either by time or space, a presence with all people who are ready to receive Him from all around the world and in every age of humankind.

We remember that Pentecost means fifty in Greek. The fiftieth day after Passover had been one of the greatest feasts of the Old Testament Israelite nation. Originally, it was an agricultural feast, the feast of the beginning of the harvest. Later on, the feast celebrated a historical event: it became the anniversary of the God's handing down of the Law to Moses.

The sending the Holy Spirit, just like the resurrection of Jesus, happened on the first day of the week as a sign that the New Creation, which started on Easter Sunday with the resurrection, has been continued ever since. With the arrival of the Holy Spirit, the New Creation has been happening. Jesus enters the souls and hearts of His disciples and becomes completely united with them. This gives to them all – to all of us – new life, eternal life, Jesus' risen life, by the power of which one day even our mortal bodies will rise to an eternal existence.

Now, just how was the Holy Spirit manifested at Pentecost? First, there was the sound of a strong wind. This is again a reminder of the first day of creation. At the beginning of the book of Genesis we read that at the time of the creation of the world the Spirit of God was hovering as a strong wind over the waters (Gen 1:2). In the Pentecost miracle, this life-giving wind, this creative Spirit is coming to us and through Him Jesus Himself enters our souls and hearts.

Then the Holy Spirit descended on the apostles in the visible form of tongues of fire. Earlier, Jesus had said, "I have come to set the earth on fire. And how I wish it were already blazing!" (Lk 12:49). Now this fire starts burning in the hearts of the apostles, actually in the heart of every Christian who receives the Holy Spirit, and this fire is the fire of love, the fire of enthusiasm, the fire of self-forgetting dedication and service; a fire that gives warmth and light to a humanity, which until then existed mostly in ice cold darkness. It gives the warmth and intimacy of love to people who had lived in darkness and the sadness of loneliness and isolation, in the bitterness of hostility and hatred. This fire filled the hearts of the apostles so much that some people thought they were drunk, but if they were drunk, they were drunk with a holy drunkenness caused by the new wine of the Holy Spirit. By the power of this fire the apostles forgot their earlier fears. They did not care whether the authorities would arrest them. They went out of the house to proclaim boldly the gospel, the good news of Jesus to the crowd gathered around the house. They wanted to spread the news which would set afire the hearts of the listeners, a fire Jesus brought on earth that would spread like flames from candle to candle so that the light and peace and joy of Jesus would be born in each heart and, thus, the joyful family of God, the Church, would come about. This is the fire by whose power the apostles were able to speak to every listener in his or her mother tongue, speak from heart to heart, so that every person would be able to perceive in the depth his or her being the life-transforming message of Jesus.

We read St. Luke's Pentecost story on the pages of the Acts of the Apostles. St. John has his own story of the coming of the Holy Spirit in his gospel, an episode that happened on the day of Jesus' resurrection when He first appeared to the apostles. Jesus came to them through closed doors and greeted them with the words, "Peace be with you!" This was the traditional Hebrew greeting, "*Shalom,*" but at this moment it meant much more than a simple greeting. It meant a new kind of peace that is much more than just an absence of controversy. It meant the peace of Jesus, an abundance of life and joy and exuberance and energy that cannot be contained, that wanted to be passed on from person to person and spread to every friend of Jesus.

After greeting them, Jesus breathed on his disciples, just as God had breathed on Adam at creation and gave life to that clay statue. This little "wind," God's breath into Adam's nostrils, is an indication that Jesus was breathing into His apostles the very life of God. Yes, by this divine breath Jesus gave to His friends His own divine nature, His Trinitarian inner life, His very self, by passing on the Holy Spirit. To make this clear He said, "Receive the Holy Spirit." By giving the Holy Spirit, Jesus keeps entering into all His disciples' lives and hearts through the sacraments. From that time on, by the presence of the Holy Spirit, He has been living in His beloved followers, inside them, united with them intimately, just as He asked His Father in His priestly prayer: "I pray not only for them [the apostles], but also for those who will believe in me through their word, so that they may all be one, as you, Father, are in me and I in you, that they also may be in us, that the world may believe that you sent me" (John 17:20-21).

After this Jesus immediately gives the apostles the awesome power to forgive sins: "Whose sins you forgive they are forgiven them." As mentioned earlier, the Old Testament Pentecost day was a day to remember the giving of the Ten Commandments on Mount Sinai. In the New Testament, on Pentecost we celebrate the giving of the New Law, the Law of Christ, the Law of Love, not written on stone tablets but written on our hearts so that we would be able to carry out the will of God (see Jer 31:33; Heb 8:10; 10:16).

Chapter 27: Holy Spirit

This is the new creation wrought by Pentecost: the sins of our rebellion against God are forgiven and we receive the ability to do consistently what God wants us to do. The passing on of the power of forgiveness of sins was for the risen Jesus so urgent and so important that He did not want to wait to give it even one day: He gave this power to the apostles (and to their successors) on the very day of His resurrection.

From all these details we become aware with gratitude that the great Paschal Mystery is indeed the beginning of a new creation. We Christians are truly created anew as a new people through the sacraments, beginning with the sacraments of initiation—baptism, confirmation, and the Holy Eucharist. Easter and Pentecost are truly the beginning of a new creation, the birth of a new human race, from the new Adam, Jesus Christ, and His bride, the Church. Pentecost is much more than a nice story: it tells of our new, restored life, describes our eternal destiny, foretells our glorious future that we will live carrying the eternal life within us not only here on earth but forever united with the Father, through Jesus Christ, in the Holy Spirit.

What is the role of the Holy Spirit?

Many years ago, a missionary in China built a small church for his new Christians. On an inside wall of the church, he drew a huge triangle to stand for the Holy Trinity. In the first corner of the triangle, he drew an eye, symbolizing God the Father. In the second corner, he drew a cross, symbolizing God the Son. In the third corner of the triangle, he drew a dove, symbolizing God the Holy Spirit. After he had finished the drawing, an old Chinese woman came up to him and said, "Honorable Father and His eye I understand. Honorable Father sees everything we do. Honorable Son and His cross I understand. Honorable Son died on the Cross for us. But Honorable Holy Spirit and his bird I do not understand."

I think a lot of us are much like that woman. We're familiar with God the Father's role in the divine plan, and we're familiar with the role of God the Son. But we're a little hazy about the role of the Holy Spirit. So, let's take a quick glance at how the Bible describes the Holy Spirit's role in the divine plan of salvation. Let's take first three vignettes from the Scriptures.

First, we've already seen how the Holy Spirit participated in the creation of the world. The Book of Genesis says that at the creation of the cosmos, "a mighty wind swept over the waters" (Gen 1:2). The point is that the Hebrew word *"ruah"* that we translate as "wind" or "spirit," is the same Hebrew word that the Old Testament uses elsewhere to designate as the divine breath, the Holy Spirit. And so, the Bible portrays the Holy Spirit as participating in the creation of the world. We may say that the Holy Spirit, in a sense, prepared the way for the birth of our world.

The second major event in which the Holy Spirit played an essential role is the birth of Jesus. Recall the angel Gabriel's response to Mary's question when Mary asked how she would conceive Jesus as she was not married. The angel said, "The Holy Spirit will come upon you, and the power of the Most High will overshadow you" (Luke 1:35). In other words, the Holy Spirit hovered over Mary, preparing her for the birth of Jesus, much as the Spirit hovered over the waters, preparing the waters for the birth of the world.

Third, a strong wind was hovering over the apostles when the Holy Spirit came at Pentecost. The Acts of the Apostles describes the Holy Spirit hovering over the apostles like a mighty wind. Then, as tongues of fire descended upon them, these frightened followers of Jesus were suddenly transformed into a group of fearless witnesses to Jesus. They ceased being a confused body of people and became the courageous Body of Christ, the Church. And so, the Bible also portrays that the coming of the Holy Spirit effected the birth of the Church on Pentecost.

In the light of these three roles, we may make one further observation. Just as the Holy Spirit played an absolutely essential role at the creation of the universe, in the conception of Jesus, and in the birth of the Church at Pentecost, in the same way, the Holy Spirit plays an absolutely essential role in the birth of every Christian in baptism as a member of the Church and as a child of God. The same Holy Spirit by whose presence God the Father gave life to the world, life to Jesus Christ, and life to the Church also gives life to each Christian in baptism by the presence of the Holy Spirit. And so, the Bible readings portray that the granting of the divine life, of the sanctifying grace to each Christian takes place by the presence of the Holy Spirit. Every grace comes from God the Holy Trinity, from the Father, through the Son, and in the Holy Spirit. The Holy Spirit is frequently called *"Dei digitus,"* the finger of God by which the Holy Trinity is touching us. The Holy Spirit, therefore, plays an absolutely essential role in initiating and maintaining the bond that unites every Christian to Jesus Christ and, through Him, to the Holy Trinity. This is the Spirit's role in the divine plan; it is through the Holy Spirit that God touches us and touches our lives. In the words of the Nicene Creed, which we profess at every Sunday mass, the Holy Spirit is called the "giver of life." Because the Holy Spirit and His working in our soul are invisible, He is sometimes called the "unknown God." Although He is invisible, the Holy Spirit's role in our lives is not only essential but indispensable. The Holy Spirit gives courage to the martyrs to give their lives for Christ; the Holy Spirit gives wisdom to church leaders to guide Christ's flock in the right direction; the Holy Spirit gives perseverance to Christians to practice virtue and remain on the right path; the Holy Spirit gives insight to theologians to teach the right doctrine; the Holy Spirit gives spouses and parents the love to live a healthy family life. The Holy Spirit is at work in every Christian in an invisible yet effective way so that Christian communities can grow and flourish in holiness and love.

28

HOLY TRINITY

In Palestine, during the New Testament times, the everyday language was the Aramaic. That was the language Jesus Himself was speaking. The four gospels, along with all the New Testament writings, were written in Greek. Yet, because Jesus' words spoken in Aramaic were so deeply imbedded in the minds of the authors of the gospels and His words spoken in His mother tongue were so dear to them, even in the Greek gospels some words and phrases of Jesus were left in the original Aramaic. But more precious than all others was the familiar word Jesus used when He was speaking about God; He called God *"Abba;* Father," a form of the Aramaic word for "Father," which was used at those times by children in a family talking to their dad: "Dear Father." In the gospel of Mark, we find Jesus addressing the Father by this Aramaic name during his agony in Gethsemane (14:36); St. Paul used this name in two of his letters: in the one to the Romans (8:15) and the other to the Galatians (4:6). But this relationship of familiar closeness to God was unique for Jesus and not shared with His disciples. Jesus distinguished between the disciples' relationship to God and His own relationship to Him. In the gospel of John, the risen Jesus sends Mary Magdalen to the apostles with these words: "Tell them: I am going to my Father and your Father, to my God and your God"

(John 20:17). And when Jesus was teaching the apostles how to pray, He specifically told them: "This is how <u>you</u> are to pray: 'Our Father...' " (Mt 6:9). For Jesus, God was <u>my</u> Father; for us, His disciples, God is <u>our</u> Father. Jesus is the <u>only</u>-begotten Son of God, while we Christians are God's children by adoption, as the fruits of the saving work of Jesus. Jesus mentions time and again that the Father has sent Him and that He wanted to do everything exactly according to the Father who sent Him.

What is this special and unique relationship between Jesus and God whom He called His Father? First of all, it means that if God is <u>His</u> Father, Jesus is <u>the</u> only Son, as He frequently calls Himself, particularly in the gospel of John. Jesus shares all, the totality of what the Father is. Yes, this Father-Son connection means that the Father, possessing the divinity without receiving it from any other, gives it entirely to this Son whom He begets from all eternity. Thus, Jesus, the Son of God who became a man like us, sharing our humanity, communicates to us, reveals to us the identity of God the Father, thus becomes God's full and perfect self-revelation. This is why, when, during the Last Supper, Philip asked Jesus, "Show us the Father," Jesus rebuked him saying, "Have I been with you for so long a time and you still do not know me, Philip? Whoever has seen me, has seen the Father" (John 14:8-9). All the infinite wisdom, power, goodness that is in the Father is present in Jesus, not like in a mirror-image because a mirror-image is not a reality, only the reflection of the reality, but in the true fullness of the Father's very being. And the Father and Son are inseparable because they are united eternally in Love so powerful and limitless

Chapter 28: Holy Trinity

that this Connection, this Love between the Father and the Son, becomes Himself a person, the person of the Holy Spirit. This is why St. John dared to state in his letter that "God is love" (1 John 4:16).

Who is God? What is God? We learned in school that God is omnipotent, all-powerful. He is eternal, timeless, limitless; He is infinite in every way. God is spiritual, immaterial, and therefore incorruptible. God is good: His goodness knows no limits. God is all goodness, without the slightest trace of evil. God is infinite intelligence; He is omniscient, all-knowing. He knows everything about all His creatures, including the millions of galaxies, and including ourselves, each human being. He knows each of us better than we know ourselves. He is present everywhere: there is no spot in the universe where He would not be. He is also infinitely wise; His wisdom is absolute. These are all attributes of God that can be figured out by the mere human mind, by mere philosophy, without divine revelation, without the Bible. If there is a God, He must be like this. Without any of these traits, He would not be God.

Now, what does <u>divine revelation</u> say about God? What do we read about God in the Bible? When Moses asked God at the burning bush what His name was, he received from God a mysterious response: "*Yahweh*; I am who I am." And then God added, "This is my name; this will be my name forever." What does this name, the so-called *Tetragrammaton*, mean? God's response to Moses is an ambiguous answer. Yes, God gave a name to Moses by which He can be called (even if later Jews were forbidden ever to pronounce this name, and substituted for it the name "*Adonai;*

Lord"). But, at the same time, the "name" is also a refusal to give a name. Yes, it is a name by which God could be called but, at the same time, it is a no-name. "I am who I am" means also that in reality God does not have a name because He is infinite being, Being itself, so that no name can express what He is. He cannot be boxed in by any human word because He would break through any word, any human concept. No earthly term could contain Him.

Now is this all we can know about God? Must we be satisfied with hearing that we cannot know anything about the essence of God, what and who He really is? Yes, we can say that we have to be satisfied with the realization that with our limited human mind we will never be able to penetrate the whole mystery of the One who made us and who made the whole universe because God is infinitely greater than our human mind. But we can realize that God is not just an unsolvable enigma or some kind of a puzzle ever beyond our understanding, since we can learn who God is if we listen to the way He spoke to His people. In Isaiah God comforted His chosen ones: "Can a mother forget her infant, be without tenderness for the child of her womb? Even should she forget, I will never forget you" (Is 49:15). God is compared here to the mother of an infant who cares for her baby with great tenderness. In Hosea God speaks to His chosen people even more boldly as a lover does to his bride. He says, "I will espouse you to me forever: I will espouse you in right and in justice, in love and in mercy: I will espouse you in fidelity and you shall know the Lord" (Hos 2:21-22). Yes, God says, this is the way, how we shall <u>know</u> the Lord: not by

Chapter 28: Holy Trinity

meticulous analysis, not by straining our mind beyond its capacity. We will know Him by experience, by experiencing Him as our tender loving Lord. God is not a theory or a mathematical formula to be understood by mere speculation: God is to be received by a human person as a Father, as a Parent, as the closest Friend, as a Lover, as a Spouse. This is what God wanted to tell Moses at the burning bush: God's mystery cannot be penetrated by the efforts of the human <u>mind</u>: who God ultimately is can be fathomed only by a feeling human <u>heart</u>. There are times when the heart is more intelligent and perceptive than the smartest mind.

Jesus Christ is our principal teacher for learning who God is. Jesus Christ is God's full revelation to human beings. Jesus came for that particular purpose: to teach us who God is. Looking at Him, listening to Him is the principal way to learn about God. Jesus was walking around in the Holy Land doing good, performing miracles, teaching the truth. Seeing this, we learn that God is good, all goodness. He is powerful—He can do what no human being would be able to do—and He knows everything, even people's most secret thoughts.

What was the ultimate motive that moved Jesus to perform all His actions, to say all His words? In the final days of His earthly life, we see Jesus arrested, tortured, and murdered. Why did He allow Himself to suffer this terrible ordeal? He allowed it to happen out of obedience to His Father's will, and both the Father and Jesus allowed this to happen in order to save us human beings. When we realize that for us Jesus Christ suffered, suffered to the point of surrendering Himself totally and giving His life for us, we understand that the most important characteristic feature of God is love. All of God's attributes are essential, *sine-qua-non* features, but the main, over-arching quality of all of them is love. When the Evangelist St. John was looking for the shortest way to say who God is, he found these three brief words to express the essence of God: "God is love" (1 John 4:8).

This is a basic text about who God is: "Beloved, let us love one another, because love is of God: everyone who loves is begotten by God and knows God. Whoever is without love, does not know God, for <u>God is love</u>. In this way the love of God was revealed to us: God sent His only Son into the world so that we might have life through Him. In this is love: not that we have loved God, but that He loved us and sent His Son as expiation for our sins. Beloved, if God so loved us, we also must love one another. No one has ever seen God. Yet if we love one another, God remains in us, and His love is brought to perfection in us" (1 Jn 4:7-12).

Love is the most intimate connection and communication between two persons. Since God is love, loving communication, then by absolute necessity, God must be a community. A God existing in an icy, lone solitude is unimaginable. A lonesome God would be unable to love. This is why God is – and must be – a community, a community of three Persons, Father, Son, and Holy Spirit. The Father pronounces Himself totally in love in the eternal present of the divinity in a single Word, and this Word becomes the Father's exact image in love, His Son. They are two equal divine Persons in an absolute unity, and this Love itself uniting them becomes the third divine Person, the Holy Spirit. This infinite divine love has been cascading between the three divine Persons for all eternity when, out of that eternal love, God created the spiritual beings of angels and the whole material universe. And at one point of human history, this Son, the Word, the perfect image of the Father put on the human nature and came among us as Jesus of Nazareth.

The first revelation of the sublime mystery of the Holy Trinity happened at Jesus' baptism in the Jordan River: "After Jesus was baptized, he came up from the water, and behold, the heavens were opened and He saw the Spirit of God descending like a dove and coming upon Him. And a voice came from the heavens, saying, 'This is my beloved Son, with whom I am well pleased' " (Mt 3:16-17). The words "beloved" and "with whom I am well pleased" express perfectly the intimate love relationship uniting the Father and His Son, Jesus, by the presence of the Holy Spirit.

The most remarkable and most wonderful feature of the mystery of the Holy Trinity is that we human beings are not just neutral bystanders contemplating it from the "outside," but by the grace of God we are involved in the mystery, we are participants in it. Jesus Christ, by becoming a human being and redeeming us by His blood, made every willing person His brother and sister, and as He is sharing the divine life eternally flowing between the Persons of the Holy Trinity, He made us, His brothers and sisters, also sharers of it. St. John calls this participation in the inner life of the Triune God "eternal life" that we receive already here on earth by the gift of faith and baptism, and we will possess it in heaven for all eternity. As a manifestation of this reality, we should read chapter 17 of the gospel of St. John. Among other things John writes these words of Jesus' prayer: "Now this is eternal life, that they [disciples of Jesus] should know [love] you [God the Father], the only true God, and the one whom you sent, Jesus Christ. [...] I made known to them your name and I will make it known, that the love with which you loved me may be in them and I in them" (John 17: 3.26).

29

CORPUS CHRISTI

There's something special in every occasion when people sit down together to eat a common meal. Sharing in the same communal meal brings these people closer to each other. Actually it symbolically unites them. Families, whenever possible, should eat their daily meals together as a family. Because of the deep symbolic significance of the community meal, it's easy to understand why the Bible, and within the Bible Jesus in particular, consistently present heaven as a happy banquet, as a joyful wedding meal. And it is understandable why the most important Christian celebration, the weekly gathering of God's people, is actually also a sacred meal, the Holy Mass.

The Hebrews' greatest celebration connected with a meal was, of course, the Passover meal by which they remembered annually the night of their miraculous liberation from slavery in Egypt. This ritual or sacred meal is still observed today by religious Jewish families; it is probably the oldest religious ritual in the world still practiced today. On that night, along with other foods, the Jews ate roast lamb; they remembered that the blood of this Passover lamb saved their ancestors from the destroying angel while in the homes of the Egyptian families all the firstborn sons died. The death of the lambs saved the firstborn sons of the Hebrews.

Jesus chose this annual memorial meal to give Himself totally to His disciples. It was the Last Supper. During the meal, Jesus observed the Jewish ritual of the Passover meal, and in the circle of the apostles, He acted as the head of the family. But in two points he departed from the traditional ritual. This must have been a shocking surprise for the apostles. When Jesus broke the unleavened bread and handed it to the apostles, he added these astonishing words: "Take it and eat it, this is my body. Do this in memory of me." And, at the very end of the dinner, as he passed around the cup filled with wine the last time, he said, "Take it and drink from it, this is the cup of my blood, the blood of the new and eternal covenant which is given for you. Do this in memory of me."

Earlier in His life, Jesus had said, "There is no greater love than to lay down one's life for one's friends" (John 15:13). He had stated this as a general rule but actually he was talking about Himself: He was the one who was going to lay down His life for his friends. This deliberate, voluntary, total giving of Himself happened on Good Friday when He died on the cross. In anticipation of His death the night before, at the Last Supper, He gave His Body and Blood to His disciples in the form of bread and wine. Putting Himself into these two simple elements, giving us Himself as food and drink, and in this way handing Himself over totally to His disciples—without reservation, unconditionally, without holding back anything—is the very act of laying down his life for His friends. This inner, mental act of handing Himself over to God, His Father, and to us was put into practice on the next day when He allowed Himself to be mocked, scourged, stripped of His clothes, nailed to the

Cross, and lifted up between heaven and earth as if rejected by both. Jesus died on the afternoon of Good Friday, exactly during the hour when the priests were killing the Passover lambs as sacrifice in the Temple. Not by words but by His very death, Jesus was actually saying to us, "I am the Passover Lamb who gives His life not only for the firstborn of the Israelites but for every man and woman." And this is why Jesus uttered these last words at the moment of his death: "It is finished" (John 19:30), meaning, "It is completed." What He started the night before during the Last Supper, or, more precisely, what he had started thirty-three years before at His birth in Bethlehem, His total giving of Himself to us and to His Father has now, on Good Friday afternoon, been completed. He emptied Himself totally, to the last drop of His blood. This was the one and only perfect sacrifice ever offered on earth.

The Holy Eucharist is a mysterious reality, the re-enactment of Christ's one perfect sacrifice in the form of a sacred meal. This is the Holy Mass, the Holy Eucharist. It is a paradoxical reality in which life and death meet. It is the sacrifice, the gruesome death of the Son of God made man in the person of Jesus Christ, but this sacrifice, this total giving takes place as the joyful meal of the Christian community. How can we understand the co-existence of such extreme polarities? We see this paradox already when we look at a Catholic church from the outside: it is a house, the Father's house with doors always open, the Father waiting for His children to return home. But high on the top of the steeple so that everyone can see it from a distance there is a cross, the gibbet, an instrument of execution on which a long time ago rebel slaves were put to death. As we enter inside the church, in the middle, at the main spot, we see the altar, a table covered with white cloth, prepared for a family meal. But on or close to this table there is the crucifix, the sculpture of a man stretched out and nailed to a cross, dying in terrible agony. Then, when people fill the church and the priest approaches the table, the paradox is there again: God's family joyfully shares the simple meal of heavenly Bread and Wine. But at the same time we are also reminded of the words of St. Paul: "As often as you eat this bread and drink the cup, you proclaim the death of the Lord until he comes" (1Cor 11:26). This meal itself is a re-calling, a re-creation, a making present of Jesus' suffering and death. We could ask ourselves: Where do we go when we enter a church—into the home of the loving Father or the place of a cruel execution? What event are we witnessing during a Mass—the joyful meal of God's family or the terrible death of an innocent man? And the answer to these questions is neither one nor the other. The answer is: both. We share both because the two, the joyful banquet and the tragic sacrifice, <u>together</u> are present at Mass, the two together make present for us the Pascal Mystery, God's love in its entirety.

Every love in its roots is sacrifice, giving of self, suffering, and death, but in its fruit is the sweetest reality that can exist. A little child, happy in the warmth of his parents' love, does not know how much struggle this love costs for the parents, how much they must give up, how great a sacrifice it means for them to ensure their child's happiness. Every tree in its roots is death, death of the seed from which it grows, but in its foliage, it produces sweet fruit.

Chapter 29: Corpus Christi

"Amen, amen, I say to you, unless a grain of wheat falls to the ground and dies, it remains just a grain of wheat; but if it dies, it produces much fruit" (John 12:24). At Mass, the suffering and death of Jesus and the sweetness and warmth of the family meal are the two sides of the same coin, of the same reality: of God's all-powerful redeeming love for us.

An intriguing idea that quite a few TV shows have explored is the possibility of a "time-tunnel" in which brave men and women go back and forth to the past and to the future into any period of human history. The Mass is the true "time-tunnel": by participating in it we go back to Jerusalem in the Upper Room of the Last Supper, we are present at the Via Dolorosa witnessing Jesus carrying His Cross, and we are present on Calvary Hill standing at the foot of Jesus' Cross, but we are also present in the Upper Room when the risen Jesus appeared to His apostles. Yes, the whole mystery of our salvation becomes a present reality. Let's enter the beauty of the paradoxical reality of the Meal bequeathed to us by Jesus, the mystery of the Holy Eucharist, and have a full share of God's immense, unfathomable love bestowed on us.

During sacramental adoration of the Holy Eucharist, whenever I look at the Host in the monstrance on the altar, I see the Eucharistic presence: That small round piece of Bread is something absolutely extraordinary and unique, the greatest treasure of the material world, something greater than the whole macrocosm; it is the center of the universe, the Alpha and the Omega of creation, the Omega Point, the beginning and the final terminus of the entire cosmos. I realize I'm in the presence of the Maker and the

Re-Maker of the human race and of the world that "is groaning in labor pains even until now" (Romans 8:22). I'm in the presence of the Stranger who joined the disciples of Emmaus and revealed Himself in the breaking of the Bread; I'm in the presence of the Friend who told us everything He has heard from His Father (cf. John 15:15). I'm in the presence of the Master in the Upper Room as He's saying the words, "This is my Body," in the presence of the true scourged Suffering Servant whom Pontius Pilate shows to the crowd saying, "*Ecce homo;* Behold, the man" (John 19:5). He's truly everything for me, the Master and the King, the Friend and the Spouse who is preparing for me a magnificent banquet of His own Body and Blood under the species of the delicious Bread and the inebriating Wine. To be in the presence of the Blessed Sacrament is a true anticipation of our joyful existence in heaven, an anticipation of the Parousia, the arrival of the Lord in the heavenly Jerusalem, descending from heaven as the Bride of the Lamb.

30

SACRED HEART

The annual celebration of the solemnity of Pentecost concludes the joyful Easter cycle of the Christian year, which had its beginning at the Easter Vigil ceremony. Yet, Mother Church enriched the Christian calendar with three more great feasts following Pentecost; each of them, in different ways, celebrates God's unfathomable love. The first, one week after Pentecost, is the feast of the Holy Trinity that speaks to us about the infinite, eternal love cascading constantly between the three divine Persons of the One God. A week later, celebrating Corpus Christi, we remember the greatest gift of God's love, the Holy Eucharist. On the third Friday after Pentecost, we celebrate the third great feast day, that of the Sacred Heart of Jesus. Let us have a short meditation about the mystery of the Sacred Heart.

When we want to identify the center of human intelligence where understanding originates, intellect resides, and thinking proceeds, we spontaneously think of the brain. But when we want to pinpoint the center of the entire person including intellect, will power and feelings, and from which desires, decisions, words, and actions emerge—the center, which is the source of goodness or wickedness, kindness or cruelty, love or hatred—we talk about the human heart. And what is dwelling in this human heart? The prophet Jeremiah said, "More tortuous than all else is the human heart, beyond remedy: who can understand it? I, the Lord, alone probe the mind and test the heart" (Jer 17:9). The definition I once heard about what a human being is also expresses well what the human heart is: the human being is sunshine and mud kneaded together. It is true: no human being is spotless white as the snow or black as the darkest night, no human being is all goodness or all wickedness: we fragile humans are rather a shade of gray, one maybe a darker shade, another maybe a lighter shade, but in any case, we all are a mixture of good and evil.

Jesus, on the other hand, represents a completely different world: the world of God, the kingdom of God. In Him, in His Heart, there's room only for goodness. He was the only one who dared to ask the crowd gathered around him, "Can any of you charge me with sin?" (John 8:46). The answer is, nobody because as the story of the temptation of Jesus demonstrated, not even the faintest shadow of sin could approach Him. Yes, He wanted to experience all the misery of our plight as human beings, and so He took onto Himself a complete human nature, accepted all the pains and troubles of being human, even temptation and a terrible death by crucifixion, but He remained always 100% God's obedient Son. He could not disobey God even in the smallest detail of His life. He said to His disciples that His daily bread is to do the will of His Father. What Jesus stated in the Beatitudes, "Blessed are the pure of heart for they will see God" (Mt 5:8), applies first of all to Jesus Himself. Jesus is the Son of God and as such, He is substantially united with His Father. His Heart is absolutely pure because it is completely and exhaustively filled with divine goodness and love. It is this Heart that we contemplate and praise when we celebrate each year the feast of Sacred Heart.

It's a lucky person who has a friend on whom he or she can count absolutely, at any time, in any situation. Well, Jesus is such a friend. He is the best, most faithful friend. He's all goodness and infinitely powerful. In the gospels, we read frequently that when He saw a person or a group of persons in any kind of need, "He felt compassion on him" (see Luke 7:13; 10:33, etc.) During his travels, the Heart of Jesus was full of mercy and compassion toward those He saw or talked to. This is the Man of pure heart, ever faithful, yet mocked, scourged, spat upon, whom Pilate presented to the crowd saying, "Behold, the man!" (John 19:5). All of us know many good people who are generous, who are ready to help the ones who are in need, who'd do anything to alleviate pain and suffering, even lay down their lives for others like soldiers or doctors or fire fighters and many others. Nevertheless, the amount <u>we</u> are able to help our fellow men is always limited, most of the time very limited indeed. Jesus, however, is more than a mere human being: He's the Son of God, and in His Heart God's entire knowledge, wisdom, power, creativity, and, yes, effective, limitless love are dwelling. Can we fathom this? The infinite amount of love of our God, Creator and Savior, is condensed into this one human Heart of Jesus, into the Sacred Heart. On the one hand, Jesus, with His divine knowledge, <u>knows</u> every human need in the world, including yours and mine, and, with His compassionate Heart, He wants to alleviate these needs; on the other hand, by the infinite creative power dwelling in His Heart, He's also able to help. In the gospel of St. John, Jesus encourages us four times within three chapters (14:13-14; 15:7; 15:16; 16:24) to ask for help in His name. In the same way, in the synoptic gospels, especially in the Sermon on the Mount, Jesus also emboldens His follower to ask, and assures them that they will receive in abundance. If this help does not reach us right away, it's not God's fault: many people are not ready to accept Jesus' helping hand, are not open enough for God's blessing. God knows what we need, yet He's asking us to ask Him for all the good things we want. Also, God does not take away the free will from people who approach us with ill will. Still, every Christian who takes his faith seriously knows from experience that prayers do work, that all prayers are heard and answered in one way or another. Yet we don't pray enough or don't pray with enough faith. At every Marian apparition, the Blessed Virgin's constant request is to pray more, pray for God's mercy, pray for the conversion of sinners. Jesus' cry on the cross—"I thirst!"—is directed to each of us. On the cross, the Heart of Jesus was thirsting more for the love of you and me, of all of us human beings, than for water.

Summing it up, we can say that the Sacred Heart of Jesus is the center of the universe where, in a single human Heart, everything is united: the knowledge of all human needs, the divine mercy that wishes to eliminate these needs, and the creative, healing power that is able to work effectively. This Heart is human. That is why the Sacred Heart of Jesus is able to show compassion because He knows from personal experience what it means to suffer, to be abandoned, rejected, tortured, humiliated. But this Heart is also divine, its power is unlimited, and because of that we can turn to Him with confidence, with the sure knowledge that He will understand us, He will help us according to His infinite mercy and wisdom, if human sinfulness does not thwart it.

The scene on Good Friday, as the tortured Jesus was presented to the crowd by Pontius Pilate who said, "*Ecce homo*; Behold, the man," reveals Jesus' nobility of soul, His greatness in giving, His acceptance of utter weakness, His compassion in sharing our misery. Unfortunately, in the hostility of the onlookers, the scene makes visible in its full gravity and depth also the dreadfulness of our sinful selves. It makes us aware that we human beings all together, in our fragile, corrupt, cruel, and sinful fallen human nature are the executioners of Jesus. This is the way that we thank Him for all His goodness; this is the way that we repay Him for all that He has done for us. This is the tragic mystery of evil: we kill the one we are supposed to love, maybe because we cannot tolerate the immensity of this love. Jesus is asking also each of us what He asked of the Jews, "I did many good deeds to you: for which one of them do you want to stone me?" (John 10:32). The evil cannot tolerate the presence of the good, and so evil kills it. The One whom we should love the most, we hurt and torture and try to annihilate the most because the good, silently but ceaselessly, accuses us and we're unable to endure it. This is the tragedy of the pierced Heart of Jesus and this is our tragedy. But ultimately this tragedy will be concluded with a happy ending, because this Heart cannot be destroyed, because this Heart is the Heart of the Son of God, and this Heart, though pierced by the soldier's lance, still lives. This goodness, untouched by evil and death, makes the "*Ecce homo*, Behold the man" scene absolutely majestic: "and He rose on the third day, *et resurrexit tertia die.*"

Our greatest comfort is that this majestic Goodness does not want to live on the icy, snowy peak of Mount Everest, far away from the world of us human beings. This Heart wants to stay with us, He wants to dwell among us. After all, this is the reason why the Son of God became a human being, that's why He was born as a Baby among us: to share with us all the joys and all the pains of being human. He did not shrink from getting His feet dusty, His hands dirty, His brow sweaty. He sat down at table with tax collectors to eat with them, and He forgave prostitutes. He died nailed on the cross between two criminals. He wants to remain among us also today: this is why He comes on our altars and into our hearts in the form of Bread and Wine every day. This is why He is present silently yet powerfully in all the tabernacles of the world inviting us. He is here, living among us and making His presence felt. As leaven, He penetrates the heart of every person who accepts Him, penetrates every family, every community, every human institution to transform them into His own image. That's why we pray, "Jesus, meek and of humble Heart, shape our hearts according to your Heart!" Let us allow this Heart to penetrate our hearts more and more, to form and shape us, to make us more noble, more human, more Jesus-like, and not only us personally but, through our presence, also our environment, the world we live in. This is Jesus' burning desire. Not only did He say "I thirst" but also "I've come to set fire on earth, and how much I'm longing that it would be already burning!" (Lk 12:49). Let us allow the fire of Jesus' Heart to set fire also to our hearts, to let his love burn in our hearts, give warmth and light, so that He will continue to do good in the world through us, to comfort others, to wipe away tears from people's eyes, to put smiles on the faces of human beings. Let us allow the Heart of Jesus to make us His partners so that in this way the kingdom of God, the kingdom of hearts, as the foretaste of heaven, may continue to grow in our world.

31

TRANSFIGURATION

Did you ever notice the miracle? Walking in a park or hiking among mountains, you can become aware of it. Toward the evening of a sunny, quiet summer day, nearing sunset, there's a short period of time when the sun falls on the scenery from a certain slanted angle and, as a result, the entire landscape puts on such an unearthly beauty, such a heavenly splendor that it takes your breath away. A Hungarian poet called this wonderful everyday miracle "the transfiguration of the things." Now we could ask the question: which landscape is the real one: these few minutes of unfathomable splendor or the bleakness of a dark, windy, rainy November afternoon? I think the true reality is the heavenly beauty because that's when the spiritual character of nature shines through – at least for a short interval. Most of the time this "soul," or the spiritual side of the scene, may remain hidden. But no matter how short it is, this "transfiguration" of the landscape is very important because only by seeing it may one realize the <u>true</u> beauty of it. These rare but actual manifestations of the hidden beauty imprint on our minds the fact that the scenery is <u>always</u> as lovely, as stunning as it is during the time of this brief "transfiguration;" that is, the spiritual reality is always present but under normal circumstances we cannot see it.

God loved us so much that He decided to come among us in person. But man with his naked eyes is unable to look even at the sun, much less on the full glory of God. He would be blinded and scorched instantly. God had to hide His glory to make Himself perceivable by human senses. Thus, God the Father sent His Son to us "hiding," as a normal human being: He revealed Himself in a visible, audible, touchable, way, perceptible by our senses, through the person of Jesus of Nazareth. This God-become-man lived among us as a most ordinary person, someone without any fame and glamour. Yet this ordinary carpenter who became as hungry and thirsty and tired as any other working man, whose skin on his palms was made thick by hard manual labor, this carpenter in reality <u>was</u> the Son of God with all the divine adjectives: all-powerful, all-knowing, eternal, and unlimited in every respect. But these divine qualities – His splendor and glory, so to say – were hidden under the surface of this humble craftsman. After He started His public ministry and gathered His disciples, Jesus decided one day to show three of His closest friends, Peter, John, and James, who He <u>really</u> was.

We all have a few very close relationships with some of our friends and relatives. The continued growth of such a friendship or love is actually a process of gradual mutual self-revelation. In interpersonal relationships knowing and loving are very closely connected; they actually presuppose each other. The more we love someone, all the more we want to know that person and all the more we're ready also to tell him or her about ourselves. We let

Chapter 31: Transfiguration

down our reserve and we start telling the person our secrets. Mutual love and knowledge grow together.

The relationship between God and man is no different. Of course, God has always known us intimately and to see how much He has loved us, we just have to look at the Crucifix. But in us poor human beings, love and knowledge of God are growing hand in hand, slowly, gradually: the more we know Him the more we will love Him, and the more we love Him the more we want to know about Him.

The Judeo-Christian faith is the story of God's self-revelation, first to the Jewish people and then through them to the entire human race. This story was going on for millennia and reached its peak in the historic event of the Incarnation when the second Person of the Holy Trinity, God's Son, came among us as a man in the person of Jesus of Nazareth. Love pushes God to make Himself known by His children.

While Jesus' entire earthly existence was the greatest act of God's self-revelation, we see in the story of Jesus' Transfiguration, in chapter 17 of the gospel of Matthew, one episode of this process when Jesus manifested His glory, His true self, to three intimate friends very dramatically. Jesus takes the apostles Peter, James, and John to the top of a high mountain, far away from the everyday world, and allows that His humanity would be transfigured in their presence. He gives them a glance of who He really is. His face shone like the sun and his clothes became dazzling white. Jesus revealed to His best friends His divine *kabod*, while a cloud, the sign of the glory of God, enveloped them and the voice of God the

Father said, "This is my beloved Son, with whom I am well pleased; listen to Him." For a short interval, Jesus allowed the glory that was always hidden in Him from the moment of His conception, to shine through His human body and become visible: He revealed Himself to His three closest friends. Not too long after, the same three men were present with Jesus at His agony in the Garden of Gethsemane: the same three friends who had witnessed His glory saw the sweat of blood dripping down His forehead. The glory of heaven was present but hidden in Jesus during the hour of His agony. Yes, the divine *kabod* was present in Jesus already as a baby in the stable of Bethlehem, as a homeless refugee in Egypt, as a child growing up in Nazareth, as a busy carpenter, as an itinerant rabbi, walking from town to town, and it was still present even then when, nailed to the Cross, His face covered with sweat and blood, He cried out: "God, my God, why have you forsaken me?" (Matthew 27:46). But this time, on Mount Tabor, for a few short minutes, His true self, His always present but hidden glory became visible, shining through His mortal body. No wonder the three apostles were stupefied and the impetuous Peter said silly things about building three tents on the mountain top, one for Jesus, one for Moses, and one for Elijah. The three friends understood the special and unique character of this revelation and they knew, in that moment, that it was meant only for them and that, for the time being, they were not allowed to tell anyone about this secret.

Jesus calls not only His apostles but each of us <u>friends</u> to whom He wants to reveal His secrets: "No longer do I call you servants, for the servant does not know what his master is doing; but I have

Chapter 31: Transfiguration

called you friends, for all that I have heard from my Father I have made known to you" (John 15:15). Through the years, as we gradually become more familiar and intimate with Jesus, He slowly, slowly reveals Himself to us. By God's grace, already here on earth we may be allowed to experience His presence in a special, strong way as a little transfiguration. We should treasure these moments because they are like prophylactic shots to prevent in us the illnesses of doubts and despair; or, like large doses of vitamins, they strengthen us for times of temptations and for the monotony and tedium of everyday life so that our faith may keep us energetic, vibrant, and joyful Christians. No, Jesus does not want us to live in constant euphoria by always seeing His transfigured self. These experiences are just momentary consolations and evidence of His divine presence so that neither in the midst of temptations, nor during illnesses or other crosses, nor in the gray sameness of our working days, should we be driven to discouragement.

We believe in the resurrection of our bodies at the end of the world. That will be <u>our</u> final transfiguration. Presently our sins, our selfishness make us dirty and ugly; only Jesus can make us clean. The blood of Jesus washes away this dirt and ugliness, and, on the last day, gone through some cleansing, we'll appear redeemed, saved, purified, transfigured, shining with our real self, and we'll be seen with the beauty as we really are: God's redeemed children, created in the image and likeness of God.

May the contemplation of the Lord's transfiguration on Mount Tabor make us realize our own wonderful transformation. By baptism and confirmation, and by the frequent reception of the

Holy Eucharist we have received Jesus Christ, His very life with all His glory, into our bodies. By the sacraments we've been inserted into and have become part of the flow of God's own life that we call sanctifying grace. But wouldn't it logically follow from this statement that we—poor, simple creatures that we are—carry in our bodies already, now, in an invisible manner, the same glory that was present in and shining through the body of Jesus at His transfiguration? Would this not mean that we humble humans are also looking forward to a glorious transfiguration of our bodies on the last day? Is not this exactly what we read in St. Paul's letter to the Philippians: "He will change our lowly body to conform it to His glorified body." (3:21)? In this final transfiguration, in the resurrection of our bodies, Christ's own glory will shine through our humanity when God will be all in all for all eternity.

32

ASSUMPTION

We read in the Book of Revelation the well-known words: "A great sign appeared in the sky, a woman clothed with the sun...." This woman is Mary, the mother of Jesus, taken up to heaven body and soul. While we talk about the <u>Ascension</u> of Jesus, we talk about the <u>Assumption</u> of Mary. The distinction is clear. Ascension means that Jesus went up to heaven by His own divine power just as He rose from the dead by His own power. Assumption means that Mary did not go to up heaven by her own power: she was taken up by the power of God.

This very word, Assumption, includes both Mary's unique glory and her unsurpassable humility at the same time. Her singular glory is shown in the fact that she is not only the lone, mere human being whose soul *and* body were taken up to heaven, but she is also the Queen of heaven and earth. Her humility is expressed in her total abandonment to God's power to be honored by this unparalleled glory. Her greatness is that she is the only human being who has a share in the full glory of her risen and ascended Son in both body and soul. Her humility is that even in her glory she remained the lowly "handmaid of the Lord."

Yes, she has been made greater than any other human being by God because she was chosen out of all the millions and millions of women to become the mother of Jesus so that the physical body of Jesus could be built up from the cells of Mary's body--that Jesus could receive His body and blood from her and be fed by her milk. She became the mother not only of the humanity of Christ but, through the hypostatic union of Christ that unites His divinity and humanity, she is also the mother of Jesus as the Son of God, meaning that she is the Mother of God, or in Greek, *Theotokos*. This is a title that no other human being can ever have as it is Mary's unique privilege.

Christ, by the redemptive act of His suffering, death, and resurrection, made all His followers God's children and His own brothers and sisters. Therefore, Mary, by being the mother of Jesus, becomes also the mother of every baptized believer of Jesus Christ. This is the great message of the scene that took place under the Cross of Jesus when He said to Mary, "This is your son," and to John, representing every disciple of Jesus, "Behold your mother." Thus, the glory of Mary assumed into heaven is the glory of our mother, and thus it is also our glory. The children of the Queen Mother are all princes and princesses.

The glorification of Mary's body and soul is a message and a promise to us, as if Jesus told us, "Look at your heavenly mother. What happened to her is going to happen to you. She is the first to receive this glory but not the last. Her many sons and daughters will follow her into the same glory." Mary is not only the mother of the Church but also her model: what happens to her will happen to every member of the Church eventually. I remember a sign over the entrance of a cemetery: "We shall rise!" We shall rise indeed.

Chapter 32: Assumption

What happened to the body of Mary will happen to the bodies of each of us; we'll be raised and taken up to heaven. Mary's assumption is the beginning of the Parousia, of the creation of the new heaven and new earth (see Rev. 21:1).

The gospel is indeed the "good news." The good news is that God, by sending His Son on earth to be born as a human being, by His Son's passion, death, resurrection and ascension, made potentially every human being His brother and sister, annihilating the curse that weighed upon us by the sin of our first parents. The good news is that Jesus, God's only Son and our brother, took upon Himself our guilt and brought it to the cross, and by dying on the cross, made it non-existent. The good news is that when we die, in death we will be united with the death of Christ, and since Christ died and rose again, we share not only in His death but also in His resurrection. The final and ultimate good news is that what we see has happened in Mary will happen one day also to us: our bodies will rise and be taken up into the glory of heaven and united with Christ just as Mary was assumed into heaven and is united now with her divine Son. The ascended and glorified Christ is the promise of our glorification. The Virgin Mary, assumed and glorified in heaven, is the beginning of the fulfillment of this promise that will, one day, be continued and completed in us.

Thus, we are not only spectators of the good news of Mary's assumption but part of it. The history of our salvation is like a serial novel: the story of Christ and the story of Mary are already fulfilled, but the rest of it is "to be continued" and we're waiting with excitement and great anticipation for the continuation of the story in us. The final chapter of the good news is not Mary's glorification. Whenever we are downcast, sad, or depressed, we should look at Mary in heaven and be aware that the glory that took place in her will take place in us. There is no reason to worry or to be sad; we just have to wait with joyful expectation because it will happen even if it seems to be delayed. Mary is the reason for our Christian optimism: our future is bright and with such a future waiting for us, nothing really bad can occur to us. Mary's assumption is a prophetic act: what happened to her, will happen to us. Saint John Paul II frequently encouraged Christians by saying, "Do not be afraid!" If once in a while we feel that our future looks bleak, look at Mary: she is our future. We will share her eternal glory in the presence of her Son in our eternal home.

33

CHRIST THE KING

In the Hungarian drama repertoire there's a rather popular play written by the playwright Ferenc Herczeg, entitled *Byzantium*. The story takes the audience back to the city of Constantinople in the year 1453 when this magnificent 1000-year-old capital of the Byzantine Empire was besieged and taken by the Ottoman Turks. The story of the play itself takes place during the desperate last struggle, agony and death of a formerly great empire. The protagonist of the drama is the emperor Constantine XI, who during the siege was fighting on the city walls against the enemy. The romantic element of the play develops when the audience learns that one of the ladies in waiting in the imperial court had fallen in love with the Emperor. Of course, the emperor knows nothing about her feelings, yet during the final hours of the siege this lady disguises herself as a man and puts on armor. With sword in hand, she fights against the Turks on the side of the Emperor and loses her life in action.

This romantic story came to my mind as I was reflecting on the mystery of Christ as King. In our relationship with Christ, we Christians all are, or should be, a little bit like this lady in waiting. For her, Emperor Constantine was at the same time the honored ruler of the empire and the object of her personal love. In a similar way, each of us should acknowledge Jesus Christ as the sovereign ruler of the Kingdom of God and as the ruler of the whole universe, ruler over the entire human family. At the same time, each of us must acknowledge Him also as <u>my</u> King, <u>my</u> Ruler, and the object of <u>my</u> personal love. The worship of Christ the King has these two sides, this twofold meaning that is stretching in an objective and a subjective dimension, and it should include at the same time the worship of Christ as the absolute ruler of the world, and my personal dedication to Christ as the king of my heart, as my personal friend, lover, and savior. Neither of these two sides excludes the other, but rather each side supposes and supports the other. Just to acknowledge Christ as the universal King without my personal love relationship with Him would be a cold, lifeless statement, like a distant, cold, rigid, lifeless marble statue. My personal dedication to Jesus of Nazareth must necessarily include the recognition of all that He is—the Son of God, the Ruler of the universe, the King of the entire world.

Let's examine briefly the rich contents of these two dimensions. The Old Testament people of God started with Abraham, Sarah, and their son Isaac as one family. Later on, in Egypt the descendants of Abraham grew in number and they became a big, impersonal mass of slaves. God freed them from bondage and captivity, and through this very act of liberation the mass of slaves became a nation, and God, Yahweh, became their King. This was a wonderful relationship: one of the smallest, most backward, humblest group of people of the ancient world received the amazing privilege to be chosen as God's own kingdom. This king-nation relationship was so close and so unique that it was likened to a marriage covenant, that highest level of tenderness and intimacy which is possible only between a husband and his wife. The idea of God's kingship was kept alive through the centuries. When the Hebrew people asked their leader Samuel to give them a king, Samuel hesitated: he knew that his nation's king is Yahweh and so the nation should not have a human king. The book of Psalms constantly speaks about Yahweh as the king of Israel.

Yet this was not a peaceful, idyllic relationship. Because of the Israelite people's endless and repeated unfaithfulness, it involved constant tension and struggle. Again and again, God's own chosen people could not resist the temptation of idolatry of the neighboring pagan nations, and took over their idol worship. This was a blatant breaking of the marriage bond. The prophets consistently called this idolatry by the name of adultery. God, on His part, with never-ending patience tried to educate His people, at times with tender words, at times with punishments, slowly leading them back to Himself.

The climax of this struggle took place when God became man, when the Son of God came among us as a human being, when the all-powerful Creator of the universe decided to become one of us and entered the world as a baby in the person of Jesus of Nazareth. On the pages of the gospels we see the process of the non-stop intensification of tension and conflict between Jesus and the Jewish leaders during the three years of Jesus' public ministry. The conflict gradually grew into a bitter hatred of the wandering Teacher of Galilee that crystallized into the firm decision to kill Him. The religious leaders of the nation arrested Jesus, tried and convicted Him to death in a mock trial, and took Him to Pilate, the pagan Roman governor, to pressure him to pronounce the death sentence. It was before Pontius Pilate that Jesus openly admitted that He was a king. But His responses to Pilate were enigmatic: he answered the governor both in a negative and in a positive way. He admitted that He was a King but he said that His kingship was not of this world. He acknowledged that He was born to be a King, but instead of talking about His subjects or His kingdom He declared that He came to bear witness to the truth and hinted that His subjects must be faithful to Him and hear His voice. Jesus' royal calling is to proclaim God's truth, God's will to men and women, and to start the Kingdom of God here on earth. Those who would listen to Him would be His subjects. But in doing this, Jesus' activity is cut short: His people in its leaders turn against Him, hand Him over to the pagan authorities, who, in the person of Pilate, carry out their demands: they hang Him on a cross, execute Him as a criminal. By the will of Pilate, on the post above the head of crucified Jesus a board was placed; on it was written the charge of why He had to die: He, Jesus of Nazareth, was the King of the Jews. Pilate did this as a mockery, not realizing that while doing it he was proclaiming the very truth for which Christ came. This is a prophetic statement: it reveals that Jesus took His royal throne when he was lifted up on the cross exactly at the moment when the leaders of the chosen people, in the person of Jesus, definitively and decisively rejected God's kingship over them.

The real meaning of the crucifixion as glory and victory was manifested on the third day when Jesus rose from the dead, and in Him appeared the new kingship in the spirit of the Sermon on the Mount, a spiritual kingship. Jesus, risen from the dead, the second Person of the Holy Trinity, ascending to the right hand of the Father, reached the fullness of His glory: He was made King of the whole universe. First the visible reality of this kingdom was very small: taken from the "remnants" of the chosen Jewish people, by the descent of the Holy Spirit and the preaching of the twelve apostles, the Church, the new Kingdom of God was born, a spiritual Kingdom, the Kingdom of those who willingly subject themselves to Christ's royal authority. But ever since the first Pentecost, that Kingdom has been growing and it has become a kingdom which knows no boundaries, no political borders. It is not limited to any language or race or nationality, and in that sense, it is truly "catholic," universal, open to all who are ready to follow the will of God. It is the kingdom not of a geographic territory but of a kingdom of hearts, just as Jesus said, "The kingdom of God is among you" (Luke 17:21).

Is Jesus the King of your heart? What is your personal relationship to Christ the King? What should be our relationship as individuals to Jesus, our sovereign Ruler? It should be a total personal dedication—a loyal submission, devotion, and allegiance based on love. Remember that Jesus also said, "If you love me, you'll keep my commandments." This love is not so much an "affective" love, a feeling that is felt in emotions (although it may also include that), as it is an "effective" love expressing itself in effects: in actions and deeds. We love Jesus (and therefore we are His subjects) <u>if</u> and as much as we do His will. This voluntary submission should be unconditional and unlimited in every sense of the word. We have to take very seriously Jesus' statement, "No man can serve two masters" (Mt 6:24): Jesus does not tolerate a divided heart, a divided love, a divided commitment. Jesus says in one of the seven letters in the Book of Revelation: "Would that you were cold or hot! So, because you are lukewarm, and neither cold, nor hot, I will spew you out of my mouth" (Rev 3:15). There is a radicalism in being a disciple of Jesus. Just as a spouse must have undivided, unconditional love toward his or her loved one, in the same way our love toward Jesus should be total and complete and undivided. If it is such, then there will be no limit of intimacy and tenderness that this soul may experience. Christ the King inundates him or her with the experience and knowledge of God which is beyond this world, beyond what words could express. Can you imagine what a warmth and closeness can develop between a King and His subject if this King wants to be united with each of His subjects with a union possible only between the food and the one who takes it, in the Holy Eucharist? He wants to be completely absorbed, He wants all separation to disappear, He wants to become <u>us</u>, wants to live our lives, share our existence, our destiny and, at the same time, He wants us to share in His infinite and eternal divine life. This is the reality, the mystery that theology calls divinization.

Let us allow Christ to be the sole King and Ruler of our hearts; let us allow Christ to take over our lives so that He will direct all of our thoughts and words and actions. Let God, let go. Yes, it is risky, yes, it is scary; it feels like a leap into the great beyond. This is the real leap of faith, but if we really believe in God, if we really believe in Jesus, we know that we can trust Him. We know that if we hand over the controls of our lives to Him, nothing really bad can happen to us. After all, this is what all the saints did and do. This is exactly what makes a person a saint. At the end of her short life, St. Therese of Lisieux was able to say, "I don't regret that I surrendered myself to love."

34

PASSION

"Passion" is defined in the dictionary as "a strong emotion that has an overpowering and compelling effect on the person experiencing it." A passion can be either good or bad. The quality of passion is decided by the quality of the object and the disposition of the subject (person). If the object (or goal) is morally good, plus the person pursues that goal with good intention and right disposition, the passion is good. A good person is passionate who, having such strong feelings, acts with the conviction of the goodness and importance of the cause, does it with total dedication and involvement, trying with all of his or her power to bring that project to success. We call this quality in a person <u>enthusiasm.</u> Its definition is similar to that of passion: "Enthusiasm is a strongly favorable feeling for an object, person, or cause, including eagerness in the pursuit of it." If the object of this feeling is a person, it is called <u>love.</u>

In general, it can be stated that a passionate or enthusiastic person has a positive and optimistic outlook on life, while the opposite, a cynical or phlegmatic individual, a person without any passion, displays a rather negative and pessimistic attitude.

God is a passionate God by His very nature. A tremendous, passionate love is flowing from all eternity among the persons of the Holy Trinity. God passionately loves His creation in general and all the creatures within it from the biggest galaxies to the smallest particles of matter. But first of all, He loves passionately those of His creatures who are persons, creatures endowed with freedom of the will and intellect, who are able to return His love freely with a similar dedication.

God wants His friends to be passionate also. To live a life of passionate love is <u>the only way of life truly worth living.</u> Looking at the etymology of the word "enthusiasm," we see that it is composed of the Greek *"en+theos,"* "in God," meaning to be inspired or possessed by God. Enthusiasm is a divine quality. Children are, in one way or another, very much like (one of) their parents. If you want to be God's child, you should try hard to be more and more God-like. This means that the more you're full of good passions, the more similar you will be to God. The more you love God and the creatures God loves, the more you are like God and thus the more you are His child.

Yes, without passion life does not make much sense. Without passion life is, if not outright painful, just plain flat, boring, dull, monotonous, drab, humdrum. Passion gives zest to life! If you live your life with passion and enthusiasm, everything in it lights up, becomes interesting and exciting. Passion is what adds full color to a black-and-white life.

Passion is like fire. Maybe that's the reason why the Bible uses fire so frequently as a symbol for God. If we re-read Chapter 15 of Genesis, the story of God's covenant with Abraham, we see that God passed through the halves of the animals in the form of fire.

Chapter 34: Passion

In Exodus Chapter 3, we see Moses encountering God in the form of the burning bush. If the word "enthusiasm" originated from the root "in God," the reason for it is maybe God's fire-like quality. Fire is a tremendous power: it can be a blessing, it gives us light, warms our homes, cooks our food. But it is also dangerous and can bring tremendous disaster. The Greeks thought that fire was the property of the gods and it had to be stolen from the gods by Prometheus so that common people could benefit from it. Jesus said, "I have come to bring fire to the earth, and how I wish it were blazing already!" (Luke 12:49). At Pentecost, the Holy Spirit descended on the apostles in the form of tongues of fire (Acts 2). The letter to the Hebrews states simply, "For our God is a consuming fire" (12:29).

Let's try to become a person fired up by God with passion! Jesus wants us to become passionate persons. Listen to what He said to the Laodiceans: "I know your works; I know that you are neither cold nor hot. So, because you are lukewarm, neither hot nor cold, I will spew you out of my mouth" (Rev 3:15-16). If I remember correctly, it was St. Bernard of Clairvaux who said that the greatest failure and the most miserable man in life is a lukewarm monk: someone who gave up the joys of the world but enjoys not even a grain of the joys of heaven in the monastery, in that *"paradisus claustralis."* Don't let the fire go out in your heart; don't allow it even to get diminished! Or as St. Paul warns us, "Do not quench the Spirit" (1Thess 5:19). Keep alive this fire, make it grow, build of it a bonfire so that from it also other people can get light and warmth. St. Bernard was the greatest Cistercian saint, abbot, and author, practically the leader of the Western world for almost thirty years in the 12th century. In a sermon about St. John the Baptist, St. Bernard wrote, "Listen to what the Lord says about John the Baptist: 'He was a lamp, enkindled and shining.' For only to be enkindled is vain, only to shine is little, to be enkindled and to shine is perfect." *Ardere et lucere* – Enkindle and enlighten: indeed, a perfect program for a Christian life!

If this passion and enthusiasm is like an inner fire, it needs fuel to keep on going. The fuel is the word of God; we have to read the word of God frequently, meditate and ruminate on it, assimilate it, make it completely ours; only this fundamental activity will ensure that the fire in our hearts will never go out. Then we'll experience the same sensation that the disciples on the road to Emmaus did when Jesus was walking with them: "Were not our hearts burning within us as we heard him talking on the road?" (Lk 24:32).

Charles Baudelaire, the French poet who invented the trend of poetry called symbolism, has a short poem entitled *Enivrez vous!* or "Get inebriated – Get drunk!" The view that he expresses in just a few lines is that man needs something in life to be crazy about—a cause, a person, a movement—just to make his life meaningful. Also in Christian life, we need what one of the Latin hymns composed by St. Ambrose calls *sobria ebrietas,* "sober drunkenness." After all, at the wedding at Cana, Jesus changed the cool water of the Old Testament into the crimson, intoxicating wine of the New Covenant, so that people present at the occasion remarked, "You kept the good wine until now!" (Jn 2:10). Also, Jesus changed into His blood not the sober water but the blood-colored wine.

Chapter 34: Passion

But did not some of the saints behave as if they were drunk or fools? At the first Pentecost, people thought that the apostles were intoxicated (Acts 2:13). Or think of the martyrs walking up to their execution while singing hymns? Think of St. Francis of Assisi, stripping himself stark naked before the bishop and his father, or preaching to birds, or making a deal with a wolf? Remember Joan of Arc, the eighteen-years-old peasant girl asking the king for an army so that she could lead them to victory over the much superior army of the English. Picture St. Philip Neri as he was playing with little children on the streets of Rome.

St. Paul writes about his own foolishness: "God exhibited us apostles as the last of all, like people sentenced to death, since we have become a spectacle to the world, to angels and human beings alike. We are fools on Christ's account, but you are wise in Christ; we are weak, but you are strong. ... When ridiculed, we bless; when persecuted, we endure; when slandered, we respond gently. We have become like the world's rubbish, the scum of all" (1Cor 4:9-13).

Enthusiasm (also called "ardor," "zeal," "fervor") is the most valuable "natural resource" in the entire world. Nothing can substitute for it. It is the greatest *desideratum* in human life; it is the gold, the diamond, or the "treasure," the "pearl" of the gospel (see Matthew 13:46), which is worth more than all of one's other possessions. Enthusiasm is the engine, the mover of the world. No real success, no real progress can happen without it. Great inventors, great artists, great discoverers were all enthusiastic people (some onlookers thought they might have been crazy). Many people can

<u>force</u> others to do things for them; few people can <u>inspire</u> human beings, fire them up, fill them with enthusiasm so that they'd do heroic acts voluntarily, make daring sacrifices willingly, take extreme hardships, tough conditions, and unpleasant jobs generously. This is enthusiasm. If you have it, treasure it; if you don't have it, get it soon by all means because this is the magic power that will change your life. It is the true source of happiness.

Yet, enthusiasm gives zest and meaning to life only if it springs out of love. "If I speak in the tongues of men and of angels, if I have prophetic powers, and understand all the mysteries and all knowledge, if I have faith so as to move mountains, if I give away all I have and if I deliver my body to be burned, but have not love, <u>I am nothing</u>" (1Cor 13:1-4). Yes, God is a passionate God because He is a passionate Lover. Our enthusiasm has to flow from love because otherwise we remain only "a noisy gong, a clanging cymbal" (1Cor 13:1). Prophecies and tongues and knowledge, they all will pass away but "love never ends" (1Cor 13:8), and neither will enthusiasm that springs out of love.

At the end of his *Rule*, St. Benedict has a chapter about "the good zeal monks should possess" (chap. 72). The chapter starts like this: "There is evil and bitter rivalry which keeps one from God and leads to Hell. Likewise, there is a good spirit of zealousness which keeps one from vice and leads to God and eternal life. Monks should practice this zeal with ardent love." Notice the vocabulary: "ardent love," a love that is burning like fire. In other words, passionate love, enthusiasm.

Chapter 34: Passion

There is in the dictionary another definition of the term "passion": "Suffering or agony as of a martyr." The two definitions of the word "passion" are very close to each other. Passion in the sense of enthusiasm and love can lead a person to passion in the sense of suffering or agony. The principal example for the coincidence of the two meanings of the same word is Jesus Christ: His love and enthusiasm for His Father and the human race led Him to be arrested, tortured, and hanged on the Cross on Calvary Hill. His passionate heart led him to His Passion. Christ's unlimited love, His uncompromising zeal and enthusiasm, His total dedication to God and men led the God-man all the way to the only logical end of absolute love: death, because "Stern as death is love, relentless as the nether world is devotion; its flames are a blazing fire" (Song of Songs 8:6).

35

DEATH

Pope St. John Paul II frequently spoke about our times as the clash of two cultures: the culture of life and the culture of death. Our secularized age is obsessed with the idea of death. During the 1970s, it was fashionable to talk about the death of God, that shocking phrase coined by Friedrich Nietzsche in the 19th century which became popular, even faddish. It was in vogue to talk about the "death of God" at cocktail parties, there was a "death of God" theology and there were "death of God" theologians. Some three or four decades later there are thinkers who seem to be ready to declare death itself as god. It's true that the thought of our unavoidable mortality has been one of the main concerns of man in any time period, but today, for many people, death dominates the entire human existence and death is the ultimate governing principle of their lives. Some time ago I noticed in an issue of *The New York Times Book Review* that in the best seller list of paperback fiction, six out of the twenty listed books had in their titles the word "death." A shocking expression of this macabre existential mood is the image painted by New Testament scholar and former Catholic priest John Dominic Crossan. He writes, "There is no lighthouse keeper. There is no lighthouse. There is no dry land. There are only people living on rafts made from their own imaginations. And there is the sea." In this image the guard in the lighthouse represents the traditional image of God, and the ocean, which besieges non-stop and finally breaks to pieces these fictitious rafts that hold the people, stands for death itself. What is suggested by the image is that, ultimately, death rules. But does it? We can realize that without faith in God, without revelation and redemption, while surrounded by the experiences of the horrors of our age, it is almost unavoidable that the human mind ends up with such a chilling worldview.

Yes, death seemingly has been victorious over everything and everybody. Alexander the Great, Napoleon, or Hitler may have conquered half the world, yet they could not conquer their own deaths. Death the Reaper conquers even the greatest conquerors. Whether you become rich or famous or powerful, it does not matter: at the end you lose everything because death ends everything. Nobody can stand up against death, because, at the end, death wins over everything and everybody. Death is the greatest absurdity that ever existed: that a beloved person with a treasury of knowledge and skills, of kindness and loveliness, of vibrancy of intellect, sense of humor, familiar glint of smile, the whole spectrum of various talents, an entire lifetime of memories—a human being, with all his or her wealth of unique personality would just pass away forever from one moment to the next without any possibility of return. Such a senseless and shocking end of a rich human life makes life itself look like an absurd and tragic reality. The unchangeable fact that we all have to die makes the meaning of our whole lives questionable and doubtful. Why do we struggle, work, suffer? Why do we build? Why do we create new things if so quickly we must leave everything behind?

Chapter 35: Death

Why should we care for others if one day we must be separated from everyone we have ever loved? Why should we see, hear, experience beauty and goodness and happiness if all of that is only a transitory moment like a pleasant passing breeze that we cannot enjoy forever? If we cannot live and love forever, why live and love at all?

Forever: This is the key word of human life. Whatever we like and whomever we love we wish to possess forever. It's written into our genes, into our blood, into our instincts that we long to live forever. We feel in our bones that we have been created for eternity. That's why the pharaohs built their pyramids, why the painter paints his pictures, the poet writes his poems, and that's why parents want to have children and grandchildren: because of their desire to leave behind in this world something great and beautiful, some part of themselves. Yes, we know that we have been created for eternity because we know from the Bible that we have been created in the image and likeness of God. That's the reason why we want to live forever, that's the reason why we find death an absurdity. We ask God defiantly, "If you created us to share in your happiness, why did you not create us immortal?"

Well, originally, man and woman were created, body and soul, immortal. But God, creating them in His own image and likeness, created them also free – just as He Himself is free. When God gave man freedom, He gambled; He took a tremendously great risk and He lost. Man and woman miserably misused their freedom. God lost, and when God lost, we all lost: we lost our immortality and so we all have to die. Death entered our world and since then Death is the inevitable end of human life on earth. And when death entered the world, absurdity entered our world.

But God is a stubborn God: He did not give up. He is a stubborn God because He is a loving God, and, as St. Paul writes, "love never ends; … faith, hope, and love remain, these three, but the greatest of these is love" (1 Cor 13:8.13). His limitless love pushed God to continue to gamble and He took an even greater risk: He sent His Son to earth as a man, just like the landowner in Jesus' parable who "sent his son to them thinking, 'They will respect my son' " (Matthew 21:37). The Son, from the day of His birth, encountered opposition. During His public ministry the leaders of the people rejected Him, and the resistance and opposition grew to the point that these leaders decided to kill Him. Through all this struggle this Son of God, unlike Adam, remained obedient; He was unwaveringly obedient through the ordeals of being condemned to death, tortured and killed, nailed to a cross. He was obedient unto death. And by being obedient He shared the plight of human life to the very bottom of it, including death.

The death of Jesus on the cross seemed to be indeed the ultimate victory of Death over Life: The great Healer, the great Teacher who said that He will bring to His people the Kingdom of God was crucified like a rebel slave between two criminals, dying a terrible death and quickly buried. There was no sign of Him any longer, His disciples were dispersed and went into hiding, and those Jewish leaders were relieved that their world had been freed from the disturbing presence of that Galilean Rabbi forever.

Chapter 35: Death

But love, divine love, can bring out something good, even out of what is the worst: death. Love has the ability to change death into life. We read in the Song of Songs: "Set me as seal upon your heart, as a seal upon your arm, for love is strong as death" (Songs 8:6). Death is strong, stronger than anything alive on earth. But the Bible asserts that love is as strong as death, and, as it turned out, it is even stronger than death.

Death's victory over life was only an apparent victory because on the third day Jesus rose from the dead to an indestructible, immortal life; this death was a voluntary death of the Son of God who accepted even death out of love of His Father and of His fellow men and women. Death could not destroy Him because He carried in Himself eternal, divine life; actually, He was Life itself, eternal, Divine Life that death could never overpower or defeat: "I am the resurrection and the life" (John 11:24); "I am the way and the truth and the life" (John 14:6). He who is Life defeated Death; He rose from the dead and His resurrection became the death of Death itself.

What does this mean? Indeed, the death and resurrection of the One who is Life changed the character and meaning of death forever. What used to be the sign of final annihilation became for the friends of Jesus the sign of a new, eternal life: the sign of resurrection. From the dawn of that Easter Sunday when the disciples found Jesus' tomb empty, death has lost its power. Even though every human being still has to die, the basic character of death has changed radically. For a believing follower of Christ, death actually became an entry into an eternal, glorious life. We still have to die and we'll still be buried and our bodies will still decay. What exactly has been changed? The event of Christ's death and resurrection changed death as the ultimate Killer into death as a smallpox vaccine. What is a smallpox vaccination? The smallpox vaccination gives the patient the very illness it is meant to protect against, but it gives it in a very small amount. A smallpox vaccine will give you a mild version of smallpox in order to make you immune against smallpox. This is what death does to a good Christian. When our body dies, we die with Christ and we are buried with Christ so that we would be able to rise with Christ to an eternal, glorious, never-dying life. In our death when we'll be united with the death of Christ, this death will make us immune against death – the eternal death. Christ changed death into a smallpox vaccination against death. What used to be mankind's ultimate tragedy, has become a medicine for eternal life.

Now, death stopped being the ultimate tragedy for a Christian. "Death is <u>pregnant</u> with life and with love because of what Christ has done for us…" (from an interview with Sister Theresa Aletheia Noble, F.S.P.). When we receive in ourselves Christ's risen divine life through the sacraments, order returns to the world, absurdity is expelled, and death obtains a positive meaning. Before, death was a tragic end; now, it has become the source of new life. For an atheist, death is the utter absurdity and the absolute tragedy because for him, after he dies, there comes the big, black Nothing. For an atheist, death cancels all meaning of life. Why should we live and struggle at all, if, sooner or later, life is followed by that big, black Nothing anyway? But for a Christian, because of the death and resurrection of Christ, death stopped being the ultimate tragedy. In the death of a Christian, as the Preface of the Mass for the dead says, "Life has changed, not ended." This is the wonderful truth in Christian life: our new, eternal life starts not after our death but it starts here on earth when we are baptized and are imbued by the risen life of Christ, and this eternal life continues to flourish and grow in us, unless we expel it through a major offense against God. In a way, through the sacraments – first of all in baptism, followed by confirmation and the Holy Eucharist – heaven itself comes to us here on earth. If we live this eternal life given to us at baptism, nothing really bad can happen to us: we dwell in the love of God as in a safe, protected place. In some sense, we live already in heaven, even in the midst of our present pain and troubles and loneliness.

This is the new meaning of death: "Unless a grain of wheat falls to the ground and dies, it remains just a grain of wheat; but if it dies, it produces much fruit" (John 12:24). Jesus is the seed of this new life and, because Jesus died and rose from the dead, the seed of new life is planted into us by the sacraments, beginning with baptism and the Holy Eucharist. We carry this new life, called sanctifying grace, hidden in our fragile bodies. When we die, death is not the end of life but the breaking out of the eternal life hidden in us by the limitations of our mortal bodies into eternal dimensions. Life is one and indivisible; it cannot be separated into a life here on earth and another life after death. Human life, as redeemed by Jesus Christ, is like a tree that keeps growing and growing, and when it cannot grow any taller here on earth, it breaks through the sky of earthly life and grows into heaven. This death is not a horrifying enemy any longer; rather, it's our ally; not a stumbling block, but a stepping stone toward God, or, as St. Francis of Assisi called it: "Sister Death." Not only is life one and indivisible, but so also is love. Recall the words quoted earlier: "Love is strong as death" (Song 8:6) and "Love never ends" (1 Cor 13:8). Just as the soul is immortal, just as the body will be raised at the end of times to eternal life, so also the love that a person ever has had in his or her earthly life will live on and will continue to grow even after death. Our departed loved ones take their love along with all the beauty and wealth of their personalities into eternity. At the end, I think, our risen bodies, with all their skills and talents, will look and act as they looked and acted at the peak of our lives, without any brokenness—at that point of life when they reached their topmost condition before they started their decline of sickness and old age. Plus, they'll become more beautiful, more precious than they ever had been in their earthly life because they will be freed from all traces of selfishness. If we think of our friends and relatives who died, we should believe that the wealth of their personalities is with them either in their already purified state, or as being purified in Purgatory—and if it is with them, it is also with us. As long as a person is alive on earth, his or her life is an "unfinished symphony." When the person dies, his or her life becomes a completed masterpiece as our own treasure, hidden for eternity in heaven. We should look also at our own lives from the perspective of death and, from time to time, we should ask ourselves: Am I really working on the masterpiece I'm supposed to become? Am I living my days in such a way that my words and deeds and thoughts keep building up in me, that temple of the Holy Trinity that God meant me to be? Yes, we realize that most of the work is being done in us by God Himself,

Chapter 35: Death

but we should not forget that our cooperation is essential and indispensable. With a simple metaphor we might say that God provides the building blocks for this temple, but our free decisions are the mortar that holds the structure together. There is the saying that everyone dies in the same way as he or she has lived. Are my actions, words, and thoughts such that they are preparing for me a peaceful death? Are my actions, words, and thoughts such that I can carry them into eternity? Recalling that earlier image, we can ask: Is the tree of our life growing toward heaven or in a different direction—or maybe it's not growing at all?

In the *Purgatorio* of Dante's *Divine Comedy*, a frequently recurring scene is when the deceased ask the poet visiting the Purgatory, that when he returns to earth, he would ask their friends and relatives to pray for them. It has been a tradition for two millennia that Christians pray for the dead. This is one of the practical applications of the article of our faith called "the Communion of Saints." By our prayers, we're constantly helping the deceased get closer to their heavenly destination. The other practical application of the same article of faith is that when they are admitted into their heavenly home, they will pray for us and so they will help us by their prayers just as we helped them on their way to heaven. This is indeed a loving exchange – the best deal ever! By our prayers and sacrifices we help those in Purgatory on their way to heaven, so that by their prayers they would help us after they've arrived in heaven. I always think: If we can pray to the saints and ask them for their prayers of intercession for us, is there any reason why we could not communicate with our loved ones who died and are either in Heaven or Purgatory? I'm sure that our loving thoughts from here on earth can reach them more certainly than our call can reach someone through the telephone. Persons in heaven (the Church triumphant) and on earth (the Church militant) and in the Purgatory (the Church suffering or being purified) are connected into a loving union by the grace of God, by the presence of God's Trinitarian life in all of us. Only hell is separated from us because that is the place (or condition) of the total, frozen isolation and loneliness, away from God, of those who deliberately and definitely rebelled against their loving God and rejected Him. Hell is not the creation of God but of those who rejected Him. Outside of that condition, all people are united in God.

As an epilogue, let us finish our meditation on death with two quotes: a few lines from Antoine de Saint-Exupery's famous tale, *The Little Prince*, and another one from Thornton Wilder's beautiful novel *The Bridge of Saint Luis Rey*.

The little prince, at the end of his visit on planet Earth, is about to leave and return to his own small planet. The narrator speaks:

When I succeeded in catching up with the Little Prince, he was walking along with a quick and resolute step. He said to me merely:

"Ah! You are here…"

And he took me by the hand. But he was still worrying. He said:

"It was wrong of you to come because you will suffer. I shall look as if I was dead and that will not be true."

I said nothing.

Chapter 35: Death

"You understand... It [my star] is too far. I cannot carry this body with me. It is too heavy."

I said nothing.

"But it will be like an old abandoned shell. There is nothing sad about old shells."

I said nothing.

Thornton Wilder concludes his novel, *The Bridge of San Luis Rey*, with these words:

"There is a land of the living and a land of the dead and the bridge is love, the only survival, the only meaning."

www.ingramcontent.com/pod-product-compliance
Lightning Source LLC
Chambersburg PA
CBHW050856160426
43194CB00011B/2175